For their help, dedicated to: Yulia Shevchenko (Russian), Kathy Hamilton (Turkish), and Daniel Austin, author of Madagascar: The Bradt Travel Guide (Malagasy).

Quarto is the authority on a wide range of topics.

Quarto educates, entertains and enriches the lives of our readers—enthusiasts and lovers of hands-on living.

www.quartoknows.com

© 2016 Tandem Books, Inc.

First published in the United States of America in 2016 by
Wellfleet Press, a member of
Quarto Publishing Group USA Inc.
142 West 36th Street, 4th Floor
New York, New York 10018
www.quartoknows.com

10 9 8 7 6 5 4 3 2 1

ISBN: 978-1-57715-134-0

Cover Design and Page Layout: Ashley Printe, Tandem Books
Editor: Katherine Furman, Tandem Books
Page Border Illustration: © swiejko / Creative market
Cover Balloon Illustration: © runLenarun / Shutterstock

Printed in China

Around the World in 80 Clichés

OVERUSED EXPRESSIONS FROM ACROSS THE GLOBE

- Laura Lee -

WELLFLEET PRESS

Contents

INTRODUCTION

Clichés get a bad rap.*

    At their most basic level, though, clichés are simply fixed linguistic expressions. Someone comes up with a clever way of saying something, someone else repeats it, and so on and so on, and somewhere down the line it morphs from a clever coinage to a stale, fixed phrase uttered without any hint of original thought. No saying starts out as a cliché. It becomes overused only because it is so useful. A commentator once cleverly defined the cliché as a "previously enjoyed sound bite."

    Your high school English teacher probably told you to avoid clichés "like the plague." (Your high school teacher had no sense of irony.) Lake Superior State University even publishes an annual list of words and phrases that it believes should be banned because of overuse. They've been doing this for four decades. Their list has included such gems as "at this point in time," "chill out," "I've paid my dues," "let's do lunch," "level playing field," and "what are you into?" (They got their wish on that last one.)

---

* A "bad rap" is a cliché dating back to the eighteenth century when "rap" was a commonly used term for a criticism or a reprimand. It is cousin to the "rap" in a criminal's "rap sheet."

Overuse is, of course, in the eye of the beholder.* We all have our particular cliché pet peeves (mine is using "porn" as a suffix, as in "food porn" or "ruin porn"). We tend to be more bothered by memes and jargon of recent vintage than we are by age-old idioms. Those are so ubiquitous that we hardly notice them at all. (An idiom is essentially a meme that has refused to die.)

Despite the "bad rap," I am here to argue that the humble cliché deserves to be celebrated. After all, each cliché caught on in the first place because it is made up of vivid, pictorial language, uses a clever rhyme scheme, or calls to mind popular literature and music. Clichés can have a fascinating and deep history. When they are unpacked, they often contain entire folktales. And unless you are writing avant-garde poetry, the purpose of speech is not to constantly wow your listener with your originality, but to convey thoughts and ideas. One of the best ways to be understood is to refer to the familiar. It is much more efficient to say someone was "born on the wrong side of the tracks" than to come up with your own brand-new metaphor each time you want to make the point that someone came into life with disadvantages.

Clichés also have social benefits. It is easier to convey an uncomfortable truth with a well-tested phrase than by stumbling

---

* "Beauty is in the eye of the beholder" is a phrase coined by author Margaret Wolfe Hungerford in her 1878 novel *Molly Bawn*.

along hoping you come to the right words. Your friend might be bored by your use of the hackneyed phrase "a stitch in time saves nine" (see p. 145), but less annoyed than she would be if you said, "Do the work now or you're going to have big problems down the line, you lazy idiot!" You feel less emotionally vulnerable saying, "Hang in there" than you would if you had to produce your own sentimental aphorism to urge someone through a rough time. For these reasons, there are many more fixed sayings about love, rejection, social snafus, and mistakes than about doing really well, thank you very much.

The word "cliché" comes from the French. (The accent mark is a giveaway.) It once meant "stereotype," which, before it was the word for a superficial impression of a person, was a metal cast used in printing. A stereotype produced the same words over and over. So a cliché was a phrase that had been duplicated again and again. You could say that "cliché" is, itself, a cliché; it is a metaphor that has been used to the point that no one even realizes it is a metaphor. The cliché's somewhat inbred cousin the "idiom," meanwhile, is related to the word "idiot." Both descend from the Greek *idios* meaning "of one's own." The idiot has suffered a terrible fall from grace. He was originally someone who had no interest in public affairs. He kept to himself but was not necessarily stupid. Similarly, an idiom is a phrase that keeps to itself, which is to say, it is generally understood by a particular in-group and references common experiences. Think of the idiom as an in-joke with a really big social circle (all of the speakers of a particular language).

Anne Sheehan, an English professor who studies idioms, says, "Idioms are unique, not only in their ability to carry meanings not contained literally in their actual words but also because, through phrases, they convey one whole concept that is entered into one's mental lexicon as a single item or idea. . . . Figurative language makes communication more interesting, vivid, and meaningful, particularly graphic metaphors." In fact, if you spend any time pondering idioms, proverbs, and clichés, you will find that it is hard to define one without turning to other clichés.

For the purposes of this book, I use the term "cliché" broadly to include idioms, proverbs, catchphrases, and modern expressions that have "gone viral." In this book you will enjoy (I hope) a selection from all parts of the globe. Although different cultures draw on different imagery and cultural traditions, you will find that the experience of being human they describe is universal.

You might notice that I took some poetic license with my title. Although it is called *Around the World in 80 Clichés*, there are actually quite a few more than that here. The number 80 comes in because there are 80 subject headings. All of which goes to show, you can't judge a book by its cover.

I was, however, a bit more literal in the "Around the World" part. Each subject listing delves into a few of the most popular or interesting clichés that pertain to the topic, giving the meaning and maybe a bit of the history for each phrase. If there is a cliché from outside the English language that is strikingly similar, I've included that variation for a bit of international flavor. For example, English speakers say, "The apple doesn't fall far from the tree" when a child is much like the parent. In the Middle East, there aren't a whole lot of apples, so the idiom there is "The son of a duck is a floater." There are also special "Around the World" phrases that capture idioms that exist around the world but don't have close English equivalents. There are also quizzes on clichés that will sound peculiar outside their native language; "False Friends" that explore sayings that sound as though they mean the same thing but are really very different; and "C'est What?!" sidebars on phrases that are so fascinating they deserve some extra attention.

Careful observers (and those who speak languages that use different writing systems) will notice that I have included the original language in some cases but not in others. This is not because I assume my reader will necessarily be familiar with French or German and unfamiliar with Arabic or Russian. I would like to have included the original language in every case (I am particularly fond of the flourishes in the Thai and Georgian alphabets.) Unfortunately, it came down to a typesetting issue. It turns out that producing a single book with every writing system on the planet is kind of hard, so we decided to focus our energy on things like the fun little text boxes, which we hope will make up for the lack of Korean and Hebrew script.

I, of course, do not speak all of the languages included in this text. So we come to what I call the "hovercraft full of eels" problem. Fans of the British comedy team Monty Python will remember the sketch in which a Hungarian tourist comes into a tobacconist shop with a defective phrase book that translates "I would like to buy some cigarettes" as "I will not buy this record; it is scratched," and "I would like to buy some matches" as "My hovercraft is full of eels."*

I trust that the reference books, articles, and translators that I consulted were more accurate in their work than the creators of Monty Python's Hungarian phrase book. I have to admit, however, that I cannot know with certainty how widely used or current a particular idiom from Kikuyu, Arabic, or Malagasy is. All I can vouch for is that it was cited in a source that I believed was sufficiently trustworthy. I would recommend verifying it with a native speaker before trying it out on a stranger.

---

* If you would like to see how "My hovercraft is full of eels" translates into multiple languages, the online encyclopedia of writing systems, *Omniglot*, has just the thing: http://www.omniglot.com/language/phrases/hovercraft.htm

THE MOST COMMONLY SPOKEN LANGUAGES IN THE WORLD

It is estimated that there are more than 7,000 living languages spoken today around the world. Asia has the most (2,301), followed by Africa (2,138), the Pacific region (1,313), and the Americas (1,064). The fifteen most commonly spoken languages in the world are listed below. (One caveat: You will find different lists of the most popular languages depending on how they are calculated, whether they include only native or also non-native speakers, for example. I have used the language catalog *Ethnologue* as my primary source for these statistics.)

1. Chinese

Chinese is what etymologists call a "macrolanguage." It is made up of dozens of forms and dialects, of which Mandarin is the most widely spoken. Mandarin has about 848 million speakers, about 70 percent of China's population. Together the various dialects have just short of 1.2 billion native speakers. About one out of every six people *in the world* speaks some form of Chinese.

2. Spanish

The home base of Spanish is Spain, but Mexico has the largest number of native Spanish speakers in the world at 121 million. The nation with the second largest number of native Spanish speakers? The United States. The U.S. has 41 million native

Spanish speakers plus another 11.6 million who are bilingual for a grand total of nearly 53 million. Spain has only 46 million and Colombia 48 million. Equatorial Guinea, a nation of 1.2 million people located in west central Africa, is the only African nation with Spanish as its official language; 91 percent of its population *habla español*.

3. English

With an estimated 335 million native speakers, the home base of English is Great Britain and it is the primary language of the United States, Australia, and New Zealand and one of the primary languages of Canada and South Africa. It is also the official language of Nigeria, Ghana, Kenya, Botswana, Cameroon, and seventeen other African nations. It is the primary language of a number of island nations including Antigua, Bahamas, Jamaica, and Montserrat. It is one of the official languages of Singapore and the primary language taught in Singaporean schools. (See p. 241 for some of the phrases produced by the multiplicity of Englishes.) If the number of people who speak English as a second language for business and travel were included, English would jump to the number-two spot or even the number-one spot on this list.

4. Hindi

One of three Indian languages on this list, Hindi has its roots in Sanskrit and retains much of that ancient language's grammar. It is the native language of an estimated 260 million people living primarily in India and Nepal. Hindi is also spoken in Mauritius, Fiji, Suriname, Guyana, and Trinidad and Tobago.

DID YOU KNOW?

Of all the places in the world, Papua New Guinea is home to the most languages. There are 839 different languages spoken there, almost three times as many as the entire continent of Europe, which has 286. By the way, more than 300 languages, besides English, are spoken in the United States. Twenty-one percent of Americans speak another language at home. The state with the lowest percentage of people who speak another language is West Virginia (2 percent). The highest is California (44 percent).

5. Arabic

Arabic, like Chinese, is a macrolanguage. There are an estimated 242 million speakers of Arabic spread across sixty countries, but some dialects are so different that speakers cannot understand one another. Classical Arabic, the language of the Koran, is considered sacred and unchangeable and is mainly a written language studied by religious scholars. A Semitic language, Arabic reads right to left rather than left to right. (Other Semitic languages are Hebrew, Aramaic, and Ethiopic.)

6. Portuguese

Portugal is not a huge country—it has just under 11 million

people—so it seems odd that its language would fall at number six on this list, until you realize that most Portuguese speakers actually live in Brazil. The football-playing, carnival-celebrating nation is home to 187 million of the world's 203 million native speakers. Portuguese is also spoken in several African nations, including Mozambique and Angola.

7. Bengali

Bengali is the second most widely spoken language in India with more than 82 million native speakers. The largest native Bengali population, however, does not live in India but in Bangladesh, where 106 million people use it as their first language. In all, Bengali is the language of about 189 million people.

8. Russian

Even after the breakup of the Soviet Union, Russia remains the largest nation in the world in terms of landmass. It is almost twice the size of the United States, yet it is only the eighth largest country in population. The Russian language's 166 million speakers are mostly based in Russia and the former Soviet Union, including Ukraine (8.3 million), Belarus (6.6 million), Uzbekistan (4 million), and Kazakhstan (3.8 million).

9. Japanese

Japanese is spoken by 128 million people. It has a complex grammar system based on the levels of status of the various speakers. There are three main registers: the plain form, the simple polite form, and the advanced polite form. It is customary for the person of lower status to use the polite form while the person of higher status uses the plain form. The advanced polite form has honorific and humble variants. The humble form is used to talk about oneself or one's group. Honorific is used when talking about one's conversation partner.

10. Lahnda

Lahnda, also known as Western Punjabi, is a macrolanguage spoken primarily in Pakistan. The word "Lahnda" means "west" and was originally coined by Irish linguist Sir George Grierson in his *Linguistic Survey of India* to distinguish various local dialects. The label is applied to a group of related Punjabi languages and dialects spoken by almost 89 million people.

11. Javanese

Java is the largest island of Indonesia and home to almost two-thirds of its population. There are an estimated 84.3 million speakers of Javanese. Like Japanese, Javanese has a system of three main registers, or levels of politeness, based on the status of the speaker and listener. The Javanese system of status markers is complex and is difficult to master to those not steeped in Javanese culture.

12. German

Unlike with Spanish, English, and Portuguese, most of the native speakers of this European language live in its European birthplace. There are 70 million German speakers who call Germany home. The remaining 8.1 million

German speakers live in Austria, Switzerland, Belgium, and Luxembourg. There is a popular myth that German almost became the national language of the United States and that it was defeated by English in a popular election by only one vote. This never happened.

13. Korean

The official language of both North and South Korea, Korean is spoken by about 72 million people. Originally written using Chinese ideographic characters (a character for a word), Korean now has an alphabet of twenty-four characters. In 1910, Japan colonized Korea, renaming it "Chosen." The period of Japanese rule lasted until 1945, and during that time Japanese was the official language and Korean was forbidden. Even Korean family names were changed to something more Japanese-sounding. After the Japanese were ousted, the Korean language was reestablished.

14. French

Although France is the language's birthplace, French is spoken on five continents by about 76 million people. France is home to 66 million of those people, and the nation with the second largest French-speaking population is the Democratic Republic of the Congo. It is estimated that by 2050, the number of French speakers will rise to over 700 million, with 80 percent living in Africa. French, along with English, is one of the most popular second languages in the world and is taught in schools around the globe.

15. Telugu

Telugu and Marathi are India's third and fourth most used languages, and Telugu just noses out Marathi with 74 million speakers to Marathi's 72 million.

THE SLIGHTLY LESS COMMON LANGUAGES OF THE WORLD

This book includes far more than just the fifteen most popular langauges of the world. You'll encounter dozens of tongues that range from fairly common to remote enough that you may have never even heard of them before. Here is a bit of background on the many languages you'll find in *Around the World in 80 Clichés*.

Afrikaans means "African" in Dutch. The language developed as a pidgin that allowed Dutch settlers from the Dutch East India Company and their African and South Asian workers to communicate. Today it is spoken by 7.1 million people, mostly in South Africa but also in Botswana, Lesotho, Malawi, Namibia, Swaziland, and Zambia. It is also the language that my GPS mysteriously reverts to when it loses its settings.

Akan is the first language of almost half of Ghana's population of about 22 million. It is also spoken in parts of Côte d'Ivoire, and it was brought by the slave trade to the South American nation of Suriname and to Jamaica.

Amharic is spoken in Ethiopia and Eritrea by about 25 million people.

Azerbaijani, also known as Azeri, is the language of the former Soviet Republic of Azerbaijan. In the early 1800s, Azerbaijan was divided with Russia taking control of the north and Persia taking control of the south. This history created two distinct versions of two varieties of Azerbaijani. Northern Azerbaijani is spoken in Azerbaijan, and Southern Azerbaijani is spoken in Iran. Before World War II, the Soviets promoted the use of Azerbaijani and made it the official language used in Azerbaijan schools. After the war, however, this policy was reversed and the use of Russian was encouraged.

Basque is spoken by 659,000 people in a cross-border community in the Pyrenees, which spans north-central Spain and southwestern France. It is a curiosity because it has no known linguistic relatives anywhere in the world. It is one of only a handful of non-Indo-European languages in Europe. The others are Estonian, Finnish, Hungarian, Sami, and Maltese.

Bulgarian is spoken by an estimated 6.8 million worldwide, with the majority (5.7 million) based in Bulgaria.

Croatian is spoken by 4.8 million people in Croatia and another million or so in such places as Austria, Bosnia and Herzegovina, Germany, Hungary, Italy, Slovakia, and Slovenia. After the breakup of Yugoslavia, Serbo-Croatian, the common language of Serbs, Croats, Bosniaks, and Montenegrins, split into three separate but mutually comprehensible languages—Serbian, Croatian, and Bosnian.

Czech, the official language of the Czech Republic, is spoken by 9.2 million people. Additionally, there are expatriate communities in Austria, Bulgaria, Canada, Israel, Poland, Romania, Slovakia, Ukraine, and the United States for a total of about 9.5 million speakers. Czech is close enough to Slovak that speakers can usually understand one another.

Dutch is rooted in The Netherlands and is also spoken in northern Belgium, Suriname, Aruba, and the Dutch Antilles. In all, Dutch has 23 million mother-tongue speakers. Both the German and English languages descended from Dutch; therefore, many words in Dutch and German look familiar to English speakers.

Estonian is closely related to Finnish and is a cousin to Hungarian. About 1 million people, mostly in Estonia, speak Estonian. The small Baltic republic has a history of being annexed by larger invaders, including Denmark, Sweden, and most recently (from 1940 to 1990) the Soviet Union. Because of this history, Russian is a common second language in Estonia.

Faroese is spoken primarily by the people of the Faroe Islands, with about 66,000 speakers worldwide. If you wanted to travel there, the Faroe Islands are a series of islands between Norway and Iceland.

Finnish is spoken by about 5 million people, most of whom live in Finland. Finland has two distinct varieties: a formal variety used in newscasts, political speeches, and ceremonial occasions called Yleiskieli; and an informal version used in everyday life called Kirjakieli.

Gujarati, a language of the South American Amazon forest in Paraguay, Brazil, Bolivia, and Argentina, is spoken by 4.6 million people.

Hebrew is unique in that it is one of the few languages to have died out and then to have been revived, thanks to the importance of ancient Hebrew texts in Jewish and Christian cultural life. Ancient Hebrew began to die and to be replaced by Aramaic after the Jews were defeated by the Babylonians in 586 BCE. It continued to be important as a written language for study of the Torah. It was revived as a spoken language in the late nineteenth century as Modern Hebrew and is now the official language of the state of Israel, spoken by about 5 million people. It continues to be widely studied by Jews throughout the world for liturgical purposes.

Hungarian, one of the official languages of the European Union, is spoken by 9.8 million people in Hungary. The total number of speakers of Hungarian worldwide is 12.6 million. It is closely related to two minority languages in Russia that you have probably never heard of: Khanty and Mansi. Linguists believe that 2,500–3,000 years ago or so, the ancestors of the Hungarians migrated from the Ural Mountain region of Russia.

Ibibio is spoken by 1.5 to 2 million people in southern Nigeria. A typical Ibibio village has a population of about five hundred.

Iceland was settled by Vikings who spoke Old Norse. Over time, the Norwegian spoken on the mainland and that in Iceland diverged enough that they became separate languages. Iceland has a population of about 319,000, and the language is not widely spoken outside of its native ground.

Italian is a descendant of Vulgar Latin, the everyday language of the Romans. It is spoken by 57.7 million people in Italy, with a total worldwide 64 million speakers in some 29 countries, including Venezuela, Uruguay, Brazil, and Argentina.

Kazakh is the official language of the Republic of Kazakhstan, a former Soviet republic. A little more than half of Kazakhstan's population is estimated to speak Kazakh. Because of its history with the Soviet Union, Russian is most often used in everyday business.

Kikuyu, one of the major languages of Kenya, is spoken by an estimated 6.6 million people and is growing. The official languages of Kenya, however, are English and Swahili.

Latvian and Lithuanian are the languages of neighboring countries and closely related. They are thought to both descend from a common linguistic ancestor, a now-dead hypothetical language called Proto-Balto-Slavic. About 1.7 million people speak Latvian as their native language, and pretty much all of them are in Latvia.

Luganda is a member of the Niger-Congo languages group of sub-Saharan Africa. It is spoken in Uganda and has about 3 million native speakers and an additional 1 million second-language speakers.

Malagasy is the language of the island of Madagascar of the east coast of Africa. Linguistically, it is not related to mainland African languages but rather to Austronesian languages. It is most closely related to Ma'anyan of Borneo. Malagasy is one of two official languages of the island, the other being French. It is spoken by most of the 22 million people who call the island home.

Malay is also known as Bahasa Melayu. It is spoken in Malaysia, Indonesia, Singapore, Brunei, and Thailand. The total number of speakers is about 18 million.

Maori, the language of the indigenous people of New Zealand, is spoken by an estimated fifty to seventy thousand people.

Navajo is the most widely spoken Native American language. Of the fewer than a half-million people who still speak a Native American language at home, 169,000 speak Navajo. The next most common Native American languages are Yupik, spoken in Alaska, and Dakota, a Sioux language spoken mainly in the Dakotas, each with about 19,000 speakers.

Norwegian, as you have probably surmised, is the national language of Norway, spoken by about 95 percent of the population. It is closely related to Swedish and Danish. It is spoken by over 4.6 million people in Norway and over 4.7 million people worldwide. Norwegian has two distinct written forms. One is called "book language," and the other is called "new Norwegian." Both varieties are used. There was once a movement to merge them, but it was not successful.

Otjiherero is spoken by about 240,000 people, mostly in Namibia and Botswana.

Papiamento is a Creole made up of elements of Spanish, Portuguese, Dutch, English, French, and various African languages. It is spoken by about 330,000 people in the area formerly known as the Netherlands Antilles, now Curaçao, Bonaire, and Aruba.

Persian, or Farsi, is a macrolanguage spoken primarily in Iran but also in Afghanistan and Tajikistan. An estimated 110 million people speak Persian.

Polish is the native language of an estimated 39 million people worldwide, of whom 36.6 million live in Poland. There are very few non-Polish speakers in Poland. About 90 percent of Poles speak Polish.

Romanian is spoken by 19.7 million people in Romania and a further 3 million in the former Soviet republic of Moldova. There, it is usually called Moldovan. The Moldovan variety once used the Cyrillic alphabet (like Russian) but now uses the Latin alphabet. The total number of speakers worldwide is reported to be 26.3 million.

Samoan is spoken by 413,000 speakers worldwide, about half of whom live in Samoa. Linguistically, Samoan is related to other Polynesian languages such as Hawaiian, Fijian, Tahitian, and Maori, but not closely enough that they can be mutually understood.

Sinhalese is the language of about 16 million people in Sri Lanka and is one of the country's official languages. The Sinhalese are native to the island and make up its largest ethnic group.

Slovak is so closely related to the Czech language, that speakers of each can understand one other. Since Czechoslovakia only divorced in 1993, becoming the Czech Republic and Slovakia, this isn't terribly surprising. The total number of Slovak speakers worldwide is 5.2 million. Most of them reside in Slovakia.

Slovenian, also known as Slovene, is the language of the Republic of Slovenia, spoken by 1.9 million of its residents. There are small pockets of native speakers as well in Italy, Austria, Serbia, Croatia, and Bosnia and Herzegovina for a grand total of 2.1 million speakers worldwide.

Swahili, also known as Kiswahili, is the only African language among the official languages of the African Union. It is spoken by 15.5 million people as a first or as a second language and is an official language, along with English, in Kenya, Tanzania, and Uganda. Swahili's rapid spread from the east African coast was due to the fact that Swahili speakers in the colonial period in the nineteenth and twentieth centuries acted as intermediaries between the Bantu people who lived in the interior of the continent and the international traders who arrived by ship.

Swedish is the official language of Sweden (officially the Kingdom of Sweden). It is spoken by 90 percent of the Swedish population. Swedish is also one of two official languages of Finland. Until World War II, it was also spoken in parts of Estonia and Latvia. Now only a handful of Estonians speak Swedish as a native tongue. In all, Swedish speakers number about 10.5 million worldwide.

Taiwanese, spoken on the island of Taiwan, about one hundred miles off the coast of mainland China, evolved from a mix of indigenous languages and is spoken by about 1.5 million people. It is the name Westerners gave to a dialect of Hokkien, which originated in the southern part of Fuji. The official language of Taiwan is not, in fact, Taiwanese but Mandarin.

Tamil is an ancient language spoken since prehistoric times. It is a native language to 61.5 million people in India and Sri Lanka. There are also Tamil-speaking communities scattered around the globe thanks (or no thanks) to England's practice of sending Tamil indentured workers to far-flung parts of the British Empire during the period of British rule in India. Tamil is one of 22 official languages of India.

Thai is an incredible borrowing language (much like English), assimilating words from Chinese, Sanskrit, Khmer (Cambodia), Austronesian, Portuguese, and, increasingly, English. This is no surprise, as Thailand is home to seventy-four languages. Fortunately for communication, about 80 percent of Thai people speak the official language, Thai, as either a first or second language. It is the thirtieth most popular language in the world, with 20 million native speakers and a further 40 million who speak it as a second language. In the Thai language the word "Thai" means "free."

Turkish is the world's seventeenth most spoken world language with almost 71 million native speakers. Most are in Turkey, but you can also find small Turkish-speaking populations in Greece, Bulgaria, Romania, Cyprus, and Kazakhstan.

Vietnamese, once known as Annamese, is spoken by almost 68 million people and is the nineteenth most spoken language in the world.

Xhosa is one of the official languages of South Africa. Spoken by almost 8 million people, it uses the Latin alphabet with the letters c, x, and q pronounced as different types of clicks.

Zulu is one of South Africa's eleven official languages, where 9.2 million people speak it as a first language. It is also spoken in Swaziland, Botswana, Lesotho, Malawi, and Mozambique. It is so closely related to Xhosa, that speakers can understand one another.

~1~
Beginnings

Back to square one.

Starting all over from the beginning. "Square one" is most likely a reference to a starting space on a board game. A related expression for starting over is "do not pass go, do not collect $200"—a reference to the text on the card that sends a player to jail in the game Monopoly. The Swedes use the expression "sitting with your beard in the postbox" (*nu sitter du med skagget i brevledan*) to evoke the sense of being stuck right where you started.

To get up on the wrong side of the bed.

Ancient superstition associates the left side with bad luck. The wrong side of the bed was specifically the left. If you stepped out of bed on your left foot, it meant that you would have bad luck all day. Metaphorically this morphed into its current meaning of being in a foul, irritable mood. The Russian and French both still say "to get up with the left leg." But it is getting up at "the foot of the bed" (*los pies de la cama*) that makes the Spanish irritable.

～ Around the World ～

To reset the clocks to the right time.
(French: *Remettre les pendules à l'heure.*) A reference to realigning something; starting over fresh.

When the head goes through, the body will, too.
(Taiwanese) If you start well (by getting your head through a small opening), you will end well (by getting your body through the opening). A proverb that is not quite as true in the United States.

~2~

Personality

Odd duck.

Someone eccentric. Comparing people to birds is not peculiar to English. The Xhosa language has "he has a black eagle's mark" (*unebala lika ntsho*). There is one curiosity about the black eagle: it has a prominent white rump. So by extension, anyone with a, shall we say, distinctive character is referred to this way.

There's nowt so queer as folk.

People are stranger than anybody. A Yorkshire, England, saying that has spread its wings since it was first coined in 1890. When Russell T. Davies wrote a television series about a group of gay friends (in the modern sense of the word) in 1999, he chose *Queer as Folk* as its title as a play on words. Even though the saying had never been popular in the United States, when Showtime aired its own version of the British series, it kept the title.

WHAT DID YOU JUST SAY?

The Dutch have a saying, "With hat in hand, one gets through all the land" (*Met de hoed in de hand komt men door het ganse land*). Does this mean:

    A. Better to be a beggar than a thief.

    B. Live to fight another day.

    C. Clothes make the man.

    D. A little politeness goes a long way.

ANSWER: D. An English equivalent is "You catch more bees with honey than vinegar."

~ *Around the World* ~

The devil's feather.

(Turkish) Used to describe someone who is devilishly charming.

Shoelace ironer.

(Russian) Someone who irons his shoelaces pays far too much attention to detail. We might say "anal-retentive." It usually appears in context such as "I see you ironed your shoelaces and polished your buttons."

~3~
Joy & Happiness

Happy as a clam.

When English speakers want to conjure the image of the happiest thing on earth, for some bizarre reason we choose a creature that barely moves. "Happy as a clam." It seems that this is only the first part of a long-forgotten phrase: "Happy as a clam in the mud at high tide" (i.e., when people can't get to them to eat them). Or perhaps the saying came about because when they are a bit open, they have a certain resemblance to a smiling face. Our sentimental Russian friends, on the other hand, say, "As happy as a fiancée." Meanwhile, the Spanish have a different view of mollusks. They say, "As bored as an oyster" (*Aburrirse como una ostra*). This makes a lot of sense to me.

Footloose and fancy-free.

If you're "footloose and fancy-free," you are joyful because you're unencumbered by responsibility. This expression has shifted in meaning a bit since it was first coined in the sixteenth century. Back then, "fancy" meant love. (In the U.K., they still say "he fancies her" to mean "he is attracted to her.") Thus, if you were fancy-free, you were without love, that is to say, single. A loose foot was one that was not stuck to the ground anywhere and free to roam. Incidentally, in the dance expression "to trip the light fantastic" (to dance with apparent effortlessness), "light" is the opposite of "heavy," not "dark." It might also help you to know that it is an evolution of a phrase by the English poet John Milton and that his original rendering was "to trip the light fantastic toe." Today this sounds as if it would be anything but graceful, as we hear "trip" and think "fall down." Once upon a time, however, "trip" meant "to dance nimbly." Even though we basically have no idea what we're saying anymore, we still love the sound of "light fantastic," so we keep saying it.

Right as rain.

Everything is copacetic. But what is so right about rain? The answer seems to be that it starts with the letter *R* and complements the word "right." In the Middle Ages, it was a thing to start phrases with "right as" to mean things were good. An early example (circa 1400) was "right as an adamant," which sounds weird as it brings to mind stubbornness or an '80s pop star. Adamant back then, though, was a lodestone or magnet. They tried "right as my leg," "right as a trivet," "right as a book," and "right as ninepence," until they finally found what they were looking for—"right as rain," and we've stuck with it since.

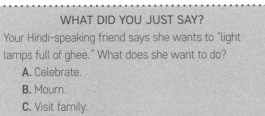

WHAT DID YOU JUST SAY?

Your Hindi-speaking friend says she wants to "light lamps full of ghee." What does she want to do?

A. Celebrate.

B. Mourn.

C. Visit family.

D. Kill mosquitoes.

ANSWER: A. Ghee is clarified butter, and it is not cheap. So to light lamps full of ghee is an expensive luxury, something you'd do only if you were celebrating something very exciting.

~ Around the World ~

The sky is full of violins for him.

(German: *Der Himmel hängt ihm voller Geigen.*) Similar to the English "to see life through rose-colored glasses."

To feel poodle-well.

(German: *Pudel wohlfühlen.*) The type of emotion that uses Pharrell Williams's "Happy" as its soundtrack.

~ 4 ~
Shyness &
Timidity

Beat around the bush.

To hint at something; to make a request indirectly. This old expression is a reference to "beaters"—people who were hired by hunters to flush birds out of the bushes by whacking at them. Etymologists believe the current saying is a portmanteau proverb, combining two earlier sayings. The first was "to around the bush," which referred to a hunting dog hesitating as it circled a bush. And the second was "I will not beat the bush that another may have the bird." The fusion of these two sayings produced "beating around the bush." When Xhosa speakers want to point out that someone is being indirect, they say, "The goat is rubbing itself against the corner of the house" (*Ibhokhwe igudl' igumbi*). In Italian it is "to lead the dog around the yard" (*menare il can per l'aia*). In Navajo they say, "Don't just deal out words like cards" (*T'áadoo saad t'óó ch'éé'in'iti*). In Norwegian it is "to walk like a cat around hot porridge," and in Maltese it is "to go round the almond."

Shrinking violet.

A timid, modest person. The violet is an unassuming flower. It grows close to the ground, and its small flowers are sometimes obscured by its larger leaves. Violets have another unique characteristic: they contain ionone, a chemical that temporarily disables the sense of smell. If you sniff a violet, you get just a hint of its fragrance before the ionone does its work. After a moment or two, the sense of smell returns only to catch a teasing whiff of the flower's perfume before once again going nose-blind. Ancient Athenians were so intrigued by the bloom that they made it their official flower and symbol. The violet has long been associated with loyalty, chastity, and modesty. The English poet and essayist Leigh Hunt was the first to record the words "shrinking violet" in 1820: "There was the buttercup, struggling from a white to a dirty yellow; and a faint-coloured poppy; and here and there by the thorny underwood a shrinking violet."

. . . .
WHAT DID YOU JUST SAY?
In Dutch they say, "To fall with the door into the house" (*Met de deur in huis vallen*). What does this mean?

   A. To be drunk.
   B. To get to the point.
   C. To be a backseat driver.
   D. To fall in love.
. . . .

ANSWER: B. It means to get directly to the point. I am not sure why.

~ Around the World ~

To wait by the sea for the weather.
(Russian) To be passive.

Warm-shower taker.
(German: *Warmduscher*.) The Germans use this expression for a weakling, and being German, it is only one word long.

~5~

Hope

Every cloud has a silver lining.

In every bad situation, there is something good to be found.
The phrase dates all the way back to English poet John Milton,
who used it in *Comus: A Mask Presented at Ludlow Castle* in
1634. "Was I deceived, or did a sable cloud / Turn forth her
silver lining on the night? I did not err; there does a sable cloud /
Turn forth her silver lining on the night, / And casts a gleam
over this tufted grove." The same concept is phrased in Thai
as "bad seven times, good seven times" and in Arabic as "no
cows, no feeding them at dawn."

On a wing and a prayer.

Trying to get through a desperate situation on hope. It comes
from the American World War II song "Comin' in on a Wing and
a Prayer" by Harold Adamson and Jimmy McHugh. The ode to
aviators was a hit on both sides of the pond (see entry "Across
the pond, p. 160).

Around the World

Tomorrow there will be apricots.

(Arabic) The punch line is that tomorrow is always a day away and therefore never comes.

The words "I wish" build no houses.

(Arabic) A much older version of the business maxim "Hope is not a strategy."

~ 6 ~

Madness

Bats in the belfry.

Have you ever had a bat get into your house? If you have, you can attest to the fact that when you walk into a room with one, it starts to fly around like crazy. The early twentieth century was an era of church building in America. They were mostly wooden churches with bell towers—the belfry. The towers provided excellent homes for bats, and the person who went up to ring the bell often had to first contend with the nervous flying rodents. Because the belfry is the highest point of the church, it bears a certain resemblance to the head of the body. Ergo, someone with wild ideas darting about in his head was said to have "bats in the belfry." This is a bit of a mouthful, so we usually just say he's "batty." A German version is "to have a titmouse under the hat" (*eine Meise unterm Hut haben*). The Portuguese say, "To have monkeys in the attic" (*Ter macaquinhos no sótâo*), and in Romanian it is "to have gargoyles in the head" (*a avea gargauni in cap*).

A GLOBAL GUIDE TO GOING GAGA

Human beings love to gossip about those who are a bit unusual. This has produced no shortage of euphemisms for various shades of mental instability throughout the world. Here are but a few:

FRENCH

Be in the West. (Être à l'ouest.)
In the right context, it means to be crazy or out of it, as in, you've gone somewhere else without bodily going anywhere.

CZECH

It's splashing on his lighthouse. (Šplouchá mu na maják.)
This is a Czech way to indicate madness.

ICELANDIC

He doesn't walk the whole forest. (Hann gengur ekki heill til skógar.)
This can be used to describe people suffering from mental or physical illness.

And the pièce de résistance:

CROATIAN

Cows have drunk his brain. (Vrane Su Mu Popile Mozak.)

Run amok.

To be in a frenzy. "Amok" comes from the Malay *amoq*, "attacking furiously." The name was applied to a group of Javanese and Malay suicide warriors. In 1516 an Englishman translated *The Book of Duarte Barbarosa: An Account of the Countries Bordering the Indian Ocean and Their Inhabitants*, which included this line, "There are some of them [the Javanese] who . . . go out into the streets and kill as many persons as they meet. . . . These are called Amuco." Readers were fascinated by the Amuco. Captain James Cook, writing in 1772, noted that "to run amok is to . . . sally forth from the house, kill the person or persons supposed to have injured the Amock, and any other person that attempts to impede his passage." Eventually psychiatrists adopted the expression for anyone in a frenzy, and from there it entered common parlance.

~7~
Arrogance

Pride goeth before the fall.

As the "goeth" suggests, this is a biblical reference, although a
truncated one. Since the early sixteenth century, people have
been saying it this way. The full line, Proverbs 16:18, is "Pride
goeth before destruction, and a haughty spirit before a fall."
This saying is found in various languages throughout the parts
of the world where Christianity is the major religion.

Too big for his britches (breeches).

An arrogant person. The phrase was first used in print in *An
Account of Col. Crockett's Tour to the North and Down East*,
1835, written by Davy Crockett. "I myself was one of the first
to fire a gun under Andrew Jackson. I helped to give him all his
glory. But I liked him well once: but when a man gets too big for
his breeches, I say Good bye." The idea of making an arrogant
person comical by picturing him swelling out of tiny clothes is

international. There is an expression in Scottish English: "He thinks he's big, but a wee coat fits him."

Stuffed shirt.

To say someone is a "stuffed shirt" is to say he is pompous and self-important. "Stuffed shirt," which brings to mind someone so well-fed his buttons are popping, is an Americanism. Its first recorded use, according to the *Oxford English Dictionary*, was in 1911 in Willa Cather's novel *O Pioneers!* There are some wonderful international terms for such a person. The Italians call him "an inflated balloon" (*pallone gonfiato*). In Hebrew he is "an overfilled waterskin." German has my personal favorite— "a lackered monkey" (*lackierte Affe*).

All that and a bag of chips.

Someone who thinks he's "all that and a bag of chips" is conceited. The bag of chips is the "cherry on top" of the fast-food generation. A phrase of recent vintage, the *New York Times* reported on it as an example of teenage slang in 1998, which means it was probably no longer trendy by then.

~ Around the World ~

He thinks he's the king of dark cocada.

(Brazilian Portuguese: *Ele se acha o rei da cocada preta.*) He has a high opinion of himself. This refers to a Brazilian folktale about a kingdom called Cocada Preta where the people have very little, but they do have a king and he thinks himself very important. There is also a Spanish idiom from the 1800s, "He doesn't fit in the world" (*No caber el mundo*), meaning the world is too small to fit his swollen head.

Blowing the cow.
(Chinese) Don't think about this one too long. It means being full of yourself.

EXCUSE ME WHILE I KISS THE SKY

One of the most often misheard song lyrics comes from "Purple Haze" by Jimi Hendrix. The mistaken version, "Excuse me while I kiss this guy," is so common that it was once used as the title of a book of misheard song lyrics. It is an honest mistake. People are much more likely to go around kissing guys than skies. In Hindi, however, there is an idiom "to kiss the sky." It means to be conceited. Hendrix claimed the song was inspired by a dream he had of walking under the sea, and the original version was ten pages long. He was known to draw on science fiction and mythology, so it is possible that a reference to the Hindi "kiss the sky" appeared somewhere in his reading. The lyrics are so abstract, though, that it is impossible to know just what the connection might have been.

~ 8 ~

Anger

To fly off the handle.

To lose one's temper. This is a reference to an ax or hammerhead flying off its wooden handle. The metaphor came from the United States and has been in use since the late 1820s, but people lost their tempers on the continent well before the Europeans arrived. The Navajo say, "He tore the clothing off himself" (*Ak'iyooldláád*). Of course, the Europeans were getting themselves worked up before they sailed the Atlantic. In Germany it is "to go into the air" (*in die Luft gehen*), and in Spain it is "you lose your stirrups" (*perder los estribos*).

Read someone the riot act.

To tell someone off, usually after someone's own anger has boiled over. It is often a parent who reads the riot act to a misbehaving child. The real Riot Act was a British law instituted in 1715 that gave the government the authority to label a public gathering of more than twelve people a threat to public safety.

When officials arrived to scatter the group, they would read the Riot Act to them to let them know that if they did not disperse in a given period of time, they could be arrested. The reading of the act was often filled with tension. In 1819, in what was to be called the Peterloo Massacre, a cavalry unit attacked a group of protesters who had ignored the reading of the Riot Act.

WHAT DID YOU JUST SAY?

A Spanish speaker says, "I'm not even going to China with you" (*Contigo ni a China me voy*). What does this mean?

A. I'm not pulling your leg.

B. The sky's the limit.

C. I want nothing more to do with you!

D. It is a negative response to a bribe.

ANSWER: C. He is so upset with you that he does not even want to travel halfway around the world with you. So there!

Hell hath no fury like a woman scorned.

When a fixed saying has a word like "hath" in it, people generally assume it comes from one of two places: Shakespeare or the Bible. In this case, it comes from neither, but rather from British playwright William Congreve's five-act tragedy *The Mourning Bride*, produced and published in 1697. This is also the source of "music has charms to soothe the savage breast" (see p. 183). As with that saying, Congreve is popularly misquoted. In the original text, he wrote, "Heaven has no rage like love to hatred

- 48 -

turned; nor hell a fury, like a woman scorned." If the number of times people quoted his lines is anything to go by, Congreve was one of the most popular playwrights of his day. His 1695 comedy *Love for Love* also contains a phrase that has become a cliché: "O fie, miss, you must not kiss and tell."

Around the World

The mustard is getting to my (or his) nose.
(French: *Avoir la moutarde qui me monte au nez.*) This is a French way of saying that you are getting angry. The image is of a powder that is starting to tickle the nose to the point where a sneeze is inevitable. This may happen after you "swallow grass snakes" (*avaler des couleuvres*). It means to be so insulted you can't reply.

Anger is a visitor—it comes and it leaves.
(Luganda: *Obusungu mugenyi—akyala naddayo.*) If it tries to take out a mortgage, it might be time for anger-management counseling.

~ 9 ~
Worry & Anxiety

Don't cry over spilled milk.
If you do this, you're overreacting to a small problem. Arabic speakers go one step further: "spilling coffee is a good omen," which means that good luck often follows bad luck. When a Russian wants to convey the idea of worrying over nothing, he uses the anatomically challenging "to bite one's elbows."

Fish out of water.
The metaphor of a fish flopping about on dry land is used to describe a person who is out of his element. It is a longer way to say "floundering." An Arabic version is "like a deaf person at a wedding procession." In a traditional Arab wedding ceremony, the groom parades to his bride's house accompanied by loud music. Thus, the proverbial deaf man would feel excluded.

Making a mountain out of a molehill.
Worrying over a trifling issue. Every culture frets about a small

problem as though it were huge. Many use idioms that, like this English one, compare a small object to a big one. The ancient Greeks said, "To make an elephant of a fly." The French have retained this phrase as "to make a fly an elephant" (*faire d'une mouche un éléphant*). In Slovenian it is the same as the French (*narediti iz muhe slona*). In ancient Rome it was "to make a stronghold out of a sewer" (*arcem e cloaca facere*).

WHAT DID YOU JUST SAY?

What does a Swedish person mean when she says, "There's no cow on the ice" (*Det är ingen ko på isen*)?

A. Don't worry.

B. Have patience.

C. Back to the drawing board.

D. Don't chase phantoms.

ANSWER: A. There's no cow on the ice means "don't worry." What a relief.

~ *Around the World* ~

Sit with your hands in your hair.

(Dutch: *Met de handen in het haar zitten.*) Not knowing a solution to a problem.

The carrots are cooked.

(French: *Les carottes sont cuites.*) The situation can't be changed. The ship has sailed.

~ 10 ~
Moodiness

Sour grapes.

When someone becomes bitter or mean after a disappointment. This is from one of Aesop's fables about a fox who can't reach the grapes and declares that he doesn't want them anyway, because they are sour. Allusions to this ancient Greek story are contained in proverbs in Europe, the Middle East, and Africa.

> **WHAT DID YOU JUST SAY?**
>
> If a French person says she "has the cockroach" (*avoir le cafard*), is she:
>
> **A.** Sad.
> **B.** Ill.
> **C.** Bored.
> **D.** Excited.

ANSWER: A. Sad. To have the cockroach means to be down in the dumps.

Beside oneself.

To be "beside oneself" is to be completely upset or angry. It used to be used to refer to someone who was insane, which somehow makes more sense. It sprang into being through a translator's choice in 1490. William Caxton translated the Latin epic poem *Aeneid*, by the Roman poet Virgil, from French. He rendered "outside herself" (*hors de soi*) to "mad and beside herself." At the time, "outside" was sometimes used as a synonym for "beside."

FALSE FRIENDS

To be in a "blue funk" has a different meaning depending on which side of the Atlantic you're on. In England it is panic or fear, whereas in the U.S. it is depression or melancholy. The original meaning of "funk" was smell. This may derive from the regional French word *funkier*, to blow smoke on a person or annoy them with smoke. There was also another meaning of "funk," which was fear or cowardice, thus the vastly different meanings of our blue funks. The scary kind of "funk" probably came from an obsolete Flemish word, *fonck* (fear). In Russia, incidentally, a "blue man" is not sad but gay (homosexual).

∼ Around the World ∼

Why are you giving drinks to the mice?
(Hungarian: *Miért itatod az egereket?*) Said to a crying child.

Cat scratches on your soul.
(Russian) Something gnawing at your heart.

To have fallen ears.
(Spanish) Crestfallen.

To have fish blood in one's veins.
(German: *Jemand der Fischblut in den Adern hat.*) Said of someone who expresses no warm emotions.

WHAT DID YOU JUST SAY?

A Chilean tells you "you have bad fleas" (*tiene malas pulgas*). Does he mean:

   A. You are scratching or otherwise engaged in personal hygiene at an inappropriate time.
   B. You are a liar.
   C. You're in a bad mood.
   D. Your fly is undone.

ANSWER: C. I would be in a bad mood, too, if I had bad fleas. By the way, if you've ever wondered about that expression, "flea market," it is a direct translation of the common French phrase *marché aux puces.* The idea is that the kind of second-hand items you get at such a market might come with bonus insect stowaways.

the actor was in and then started to play a game where they tried to see if they could link him to every other film actor in only six jumps. It caught on, and the "degrees of Bacon" game is now popular with people trying to see how many jumps it takes to link themselves to a famous person. More recently, scientists have suggested that in the era of social networking everyone is now connected to every other person on earth through only three and a half intermediaries.

~ Around the World ~

The grape gets darker as it looks at the other grapes.
(Turkish: *Üzüm üzüme baka baka kararır.*) You take on the habits of the people with whom you associate.

The corner of my liver.
(Turkish: *Ciğerimin köşesi.*) Used to describe someone who is very close to the speaker.

I see the sun on your back.
(Kazakh) Praise for another person. I am alive because of you.

To be left with only one's nose.
(Russian) To be neglected or excluded.

Eating the closed-door soup.

(Chinese) Being turned away or not invited to a party or gathering.

> ## C'EST WHAT?!
>
> ### THE HEN SEES THE SNAKE'S FEET, AND THE SNAKE SEES THE HEN'S BOOBS.
>
> There is something extremely odd about this Thai phrase. First, snakes don't have feet. Second, hens don't have boobs. What is going on here? Apparently, it refers to two people who know each other's secrets. Do you suppose this means Thai snakes really do have feet and they go running around at night when no one is looking?
>
> Incidentally, Croatians say "swan's balls" (*muda labudova*) to refer to something impossible. The interesting thing about this is that unlike hen's boobs, swans, indeed, have testes. They're just hidden inside.

~ 12 ~

Love & Courtship

A fifth (or third) wheel.

An unnecessary and unwelcome addition, usually used when a couple would very much like to ditch a friend who is tagging along. In 1631 the English dramatist Thomas Dekker wrote a book in which he referred to "a running chariot a fifth wheel." The third version came about later as the expression started to focus on unwelcome dating companions: a third party in the superfluous wheel scenario. Despite its age, the phrase didn't catch on in a big way until 1902. When Russians want to say something is useless, they turn to a similar image, using the phrase "like a fifth foot on a dog."

What's a nice girl like you doing in a place like this?

This pickup line is such a cliché that it is used only with the tongue planted firmly in the cheek. A famous Japanese pickup line is "This time next year, let's be laughing together." Nice.

Apple of my eye.

One's beloved. This springs, in a roundabout way, from a liberal translation of the Old Testament by Renaissance scholars. In its biblical context, the apple means the eye's pupil, and so, the "apple of the eye" in the metaphorical sense is someone who makes the pupils dilate when you look at him. In this biblical context, it is always used to signify something that needs to be watched carefully. The original biblical languages, of course, do not refer to the "apple," because apples do not grow in the Middle East. Today, it is applied both to lovers and to children and usually implies not only love but a bit of pride as well. A similar phrase in Spanish is "to be someone's right eye" (*ser el ojo derecho de alguien*).

Head over heels in love.

To fall "head over heels" is to be completely and utterly enamored. The weird thing about this is that, anatomically speaking, the head is pretty much always over the heels. The German version of this phrase does a better job capturing the topsy-turvy nature of love. They say, "To fall neck over head in love." Other Europeans measure love by other parts of the head; in Bulgaria and Finland they say "up to the ears" in love. In Sweden it is "over the ears."

INSTANT ATTRACTION

"Dry firewood meets a flame," the Chinese say. It's what the French describe as "a bolt of lightning." English speakers sometimes borrow the saying in its original French "*coup de foudre*." Bulgarians say, "The blind Sunday hit me" (*Udari me sliapata nedelia*), where blindness is a reference to Cupid. Why Sunday? No one really knows.

When you're struck by that emotion in the Middle East, you might "make sheep's eyes" at your beloved. The Arabic-speaking world is apparently home to particularly amorous sheep. Such a look might make "a flame come out of one's face" in Japan. That means "to blush."

~ Around the World ~

Like water for chocolate.

(Latin American Spanish: *Como agua para chocolate*.)
This cliché is best known to English speakers as the title of Laura Esquivel's novel. It refers to the boiling point of one's passion—whether love or anger. It refers to water being heated to make hot chocolate. In Mexico you do this by heating water until it is just about to boil and then pour it on the chocolate.

Swallowed like a postman's sock.

(Colombian Spanish: *Tragado como media de cartero*.)

Bleecchh! Would you believe this Colombian Spanish phrase means to be hopelessly in love? This one needs a bit of explanation. "Swallowed" (tardago) is slang for being in love. It's like being completely drowned or enveloped by the emotion. But why socks? Imagine a postman doing his rounds, walking from box to box wearing old socks that have lost their elastic. The socks keep tumbling down around his ankles, and he keeps pulling them back up, but it is no use. That's what love is like, say the Colombians.

ON THE OTHER HAND . . .

For every proverb or idiom, there is an equal and opposite idiom, especially when it comes to love. For instance, we can't decide whether a vacation from a loved one makes you yearn even more—absence makes the heart grow fonder—or whether it just makes him easy to forget—out of sight, out of mind. Perhaps the Russians can offer a clue. They call a two-year stint in the military "a cure for love."

~ 13 ~
Marriage

Pop the question.

To "pop" (meaning to blurt out) a question goes back to the eighteenth century. It had nothing specifically to do with marriage back then, though. For example, this 1725 citation from the *Oxford English Dictionary* is clearly not proposing a ménage à trois: "Dear Governor and Governess, the boy here having given me leave to ask you how you do, I have made bold to pop the question to you." It was not until the 1930s that "popping the question" was wedded to marriage.

Shotgun wedding.

As much as some proud owners love their guns, no one that I know of has ever tried to marry one. A shotgun is a weapon that fires a load of shot rather than a single bullet. It is not good for precise marksmanship, but it was an invaluable thing to have in the Old West. If you needed to quickly respond to a pack of wild animals, you wanted a weapon that you could point in the general direction of the danger and have a good chance of hitting something. Every rancher had a shotgun, and so the word came to be applied to anything done under duress. So a "shotgun wedding" usually means one in which the bride is pregnant, forcing the father to "make an honest woman of her." Of course pregnancy before marriage is not limited to the Wild West. The Japanese use the more literal term "a got pregnant wedding" (*dekichatta kekkon*). The image here is not of an outraged parent forcing the issue; in tone, it is more along the lines of "Well, I guess we might as well get married."

MISS BOSSY PANTS

Around the world there are far more idioms describing a woman who dominates a man than the other way around. In English a strong woman is said to "wear the pants" in the family. Meanwhile, in Spanish a man who is "henpecked" has "oversized pants." In Hindi they say "the wind from a woman's shawl strikes" when a man follows his wife's command. His German counterpart is said to "stand under the slipper." In Russia he is "under his wife's shoe." At least he is not "under the wife's buttocks," as he is in Japan. A man dominating his wife has historically passed without comment. The Germans, however, do have a term for a submissive wife; they call her "the cricket on the stove."

To wear the pants (trousers) in the family.

This is something of a language fossil. These days women are nearly as likely to wear slacks as men. Back in the day, however, it was simply not done, and a woman who wore the trousers was taking the role of the man. The expression comes to us from German (*die Hosen anhaben*).

Around the World

My half orange.

(Spanish: *Mi media naranja*.) Spouse. "My better half."

May you grow old on one pillow.

(Turkish: *Bir yastıkta kocayın*.) A traditional blessing for the bride and groom.

When going to sea, pray once; when going to war, pray twice; when going to be married, pray three times.

(Polish) Only one of these adventures is a lifelong commitment.

If you marry a monkey for money, the money will vanish and the monkey will remain a monkey.

(Arabic) Don't marry for money.

LIKE A KNIFE

In Western pop music, lyrics about love and knives are plentiful. Usually they are trying to say "love hurts." A Korean phrase uses the image of a knife in an entirely different way. A fight between a husband and a wife, they say, is "like cutting water with a knife." However heated a conflict between members of a family may be, they can't be separated. This calls to mind the marriage vow (which is taken from the New Testament), "What therefore God hath joined together, let not man put asunder." In this Western version it is a command, but in the Korean conception it simply can't be done—a family is one substance. (Would it be entirely unromantic of me to mention that a group of scientists at the University of Arizona recently conducted an experiment in which they cut through a droplet of water with a specially designed knife?)

~ 14 ~

Sex

Know someone in the biblical sense.

To have sex with someone. Euphemisms for sex have probably been with us since the beginning of time. The ancient Hebrews used the euphemism "to know," which found its way into biblical texts like Genesis where it was literally translated into the King James Bible as "And Adam knew Eve his wife; and she conceived . . ." Other Hebrew euphemisms that translators must wrestle with include "to cover your feet," meaning to go to the bathroom, and "the way of women" for menstruation. Fortunately, "cover your feet in the biblical sense" has not made its way into English.

Oldest profession.

Prostitution. You can blame the English writer Rudyard Kipling for this one. His 1888 story "In Black and White" begins, "Lalun is a member of the most ancient profession in the world." Lalun was a prostitute. In the early 1900s, Kipling's story became part of a larger debate over how to deal with prostitution. It was widely cited and misquoted until it became the fixed phrase we know today. In Kipling's day, practitioners of this profession were referred to euphemistically as "public women." In Spain the same term, "*mujer pública*," is still in use.

DOING THE, UM, YOU KNOW . . .

In France a person who is in the mood for sex is said to have "a yawning mussel" (*avoir la moule qui bâille*). Maybe this is why we say "happy as a clam"? (See *Happy as a clam* on p. 33.) The Japanese recognize a particular difference between men, and women's arousal in their expressions for solo sex. They call the male version "a thousand rubs." The female version is "ten thousand rubs."

~ 15 ~
Family

Apple doesn't fall far from the tree.

Like father, like son. This seems to have a Germanic or Eastern European origin. Russians say the exact same thing, as do the Germans (*der Apfel fällt nicht weit von Stamm*). They even speak of apples the same way in Iceland (*eplit fellr ekki lánt frá eikinn*). George Henry Barrow, an English author and world traveler, believed this cliché originated in Denmark. He wrote in 1843, "'The apple,' as the Danes say, 'had not fallen far from the tree'; the imp was in every respect the counterpart of the father." There aren't that many apples in the Middle East, so an Arabic way to convey this idea is "the son of a duck is a floater." In Japanese it is "the child of a frog is a frog." And in Spanish it is "from such a pole such a splinter" (*de tal palo tal astilla*).

Black sheep.

The wool of a black sheep is much harder to dye than that of his white brethren. Fortunately for shepherds, there are not a lot of them. Unfortunately for shepherds, that meant there were not enough to have a separate market for black wool, and therefore black sheep were practically worthless. Thus the black sheep became a metaphor for the member of the family you sort of wish were related to someone else, usually because they are poorly behaved and bring shame upon your good name. Croatians say, "We see whose mother is spinning black wool" (*Da vidimo čija majka crnu vunu prede*).

It happens in the best of families.

My father used to use this expression as an answer to mild gaffes. It means things happen. A Portuguese version is "Accidents happen in the best regulated families" (*Coias piores acontecem nas melhores familias*).

~ Around the World ~

To the raven's eye, its chicks look like falcons.

(Turkish: *Kuzguna yavrusu şahin görünür.*) Children all look wonderful to their mothers.

The sleep of the child is advantageous to the mother.

(Tamil) Especially when they are sleeping.

He who is not listening to his parents is listening to dog's skin.

(Polish: *Kto nie slucha Ojca i Matki, ten sie slucha psiej skory.*) Listen to your parents or you're going to have to learn the hard way.

Do not boast about your wealth if you are a father of a son.

(Malagasy: *Aza midera harena, fa niter-day.*) In Madagascar, family is more important than money. This also has a sense of "you can't take it with you," as the son will inherit from the father, and therefore the father is only the caretaker of the wealth.

Y TU MAMÁ TAMBIÉN

Spanish has more than its fair share of idioms involving mothers. There is "To throw mothers" (*echar madres*), meaning "to swear," "to dis-mother" (*desmadrarse*), meaning "go wild" or "to beat up," to "give the mother" (*dar en el madre*), meaning "to hit someone where he is vulnerable," and "I've reached motherliness" (*Ya estoy hasta la madre*), meaning "I'm sick and tired of it."

"Y tu mamá también" (and your mother, too) came into English speakers' consciousness as the title of a 2001 Mexican film starring Gael García Bernal and Diego Luna. It is the response you would shout back to someone who "threw mothers at you."

WHAT DID YOU JUST SAY?

Akmaral Mukan, author of *A Learner's Dictionary of Kazakh Idioms*, wrote the following dialogue: "Kazakh man greets his neighbor: 'Are your souls and livestock well?' The neighbor replies: 'Well. Are your black spheres feeling better?'" The first greeting is understandable enough, but what are the black spheres?

A. Parents.

B. Children.

C. Hands, worn from too much manual labor.

D. Eyes, referring to someone who has suffered a headache.

ANSWER: B. It seems "black spheres" is a Kazakh way of referring to small, cute children.

~ 16 ~
Home

A man's home is his castle.

In England: "An Englishman's home is his castle." It means that every man is a little king under his own roof. (Yet for some reason he still wants to have a "man cave" inside it.) This saying has been around since the days when it was spelled "youre house is youre Castell." It became part of English law in the seventeenth century that no one could enter a man's home (and it was then a *man's* home) unless invited. In 1628 Sir Edward Coke (pronounced Cook), in *The Institutes of the Laws of England*, wrote: "For a man's house is his castle, *et domus sua cuique est tutissimum refugium* [and each man's home is his safest refuge]."

(Oh, Auntie Em) There's no place like home.

This is what Dorothy said when she clicked her heels together to transport her from Oz back to her home in Kansas. Even though Oz was in brilliant Technicolor and Kansas was in black and white, Dorothy preferred the old homestead. The *Wizard of*

Oz version might have been inspired by the song "Home Sweet Home" by American playwright John Howard Payne, which includes the lyric "Be it ever so humble there's no place like home" and wraps up with "There's no place like home." (When I lived in France as an exchange student, the mother of my host family used to laugh at this saying, which she jokingly translated literally as "House, Sugared House.") Those lyrics were, in turn, inspired by a proverb that dates back to the sixteenth century. "Home is home, though it's never so homely." A Chinese way of expressing this thought is "Not the golden corner nor the silvery corner is as good as the dog corner of home."

FALSE FRIENDS

"Homely" is one of those words that throws a spanner in the works of communication between Americans and Brits. In England this word means what it sounds like it should, "homelike." In the United States it means "ugly."

~ *Around the World* ~

A chicken that has left will return to its pen in due time.

(Korean) In Korea it seems they have homing chickens. This expression is not to be confused with the English expression "chickens coming home to roost," which refers to bad things that return to the person who unleashed them. That saying dates back to the time of Chaucer.

The happy pot-washtub in my home.

(Japanese) This one may need a bit of explanation. The idea is that even if someone is so poor that he only has a pot to use as a washtub, home is the happiest place to be.

~ 17 ~
Vices & Misdeeds

Paint the town red.

To have a rowdy night on the town. The expression can be traced back to one famous bender that happened in 1837. The Marquis of Waterford, that rogue, invited a group of friends for a night of entertainment in the town of Melton Mowbray, Ireland. The aristocratic lads forgot that they were gentlemen and pulled knockers off doors, knocked over flowerpots, and broke windows. Admiring their handiwork, they decided to take it one step further. They found a pot of red paint and literally painted the town red. Their targets included the doors of houses, a tollgate, and a statue of a swan.

Sow your wild oats.

To enjoy a period of self-indulgent vice, usually associated with young men before they settle down and marry. Young men have been doing this for at least four hundred years, for that is how long the phrase has been in use. "That wilfull and unruly age,

HOW DO YOU SLEEP?

You may be able to commit a crime and not get caught, but your conscience (assuming you have one) will not be so kind. Throughout the world, there are sayings that evoke the restless nights of the guilty.

IBIBIO

It is a thief who is always afraid of the night's drum.
The drum, in this case, is an alarm, an early version of a police siren.

CHINESE

If one does not do anything one is ashamed of, one is not afraid that a ghost will knock on the door at midnight.
The ghost, in this case, is a supernatural version of a policeman.

KOREAN

A thief sleeps in a crouching position, and the man robbed by the thief sleeps flat on his back.
No alarms, police, or hauntings, just a guilty conscience.

which lacketh rypenes and discretion, and (as wee saye) hath not sowed all theyr wyeld Oates" (from the 1576 Dutch book *Touchstone of Complexions*). Unlike cultivated oats, wild oats are a weed that spreads easily and is hard to eradicate. So it is a bit like saying "to sow mustard grass." Basically, careless and reckless young men throw the seeds around willy-nilly with no concern over what will grow later.

Don't wash your dirty linen in public.

Don't expose your personal stuff. The phrase entered the English language in 1867 in English novelist Anthony Trollope's *The Last Chronicle of Barset*. But he borrowed an old French proverb "one must wash his dirty laundry in private" (*il faut lever son linge sale en famille*).

Love the sinner, hate the sin.

Many people wrongly believe this is a biblical verse. (See "God helps those who help themselves" on p. 105 for another nonbiblical verse.) It is often attributed to Saint Augustine, but what he actually wrote was "With love for mankind and hatred of sins" (*Cum dilectione hominum et odio vitiorum*). The expression has been with us for a while. The *Guardian* in 1898 described a traveling minister by saying, "'Love the sinner; hate the sin' has been his lordship's guiding principle, as witness the keen personal interest he has taken in the establishment of Magdalene asylums and in every charitable work to lead people into the right way . . ." The quotes around the saying suggest it was already well-known at the time. In 1914 the *Chanute*

Daily Tribune of Kansas reported on a Methodist Conference and printed the following poem:

Cry aloud, condemn the wrong.
Love the sinner, hate the sin;
Garrisoned in Christ be strong
Victory in defeat to win.
Be a master, not a tool,
Preach the Word, rebuke, exhort:
Break the tyrant Mammon's rule,
Scale his ramparts, seize his fort.

The saying really started to gain traction in the late 1980s and early 1990s when it became applied almost exclusively to the issue of LGBT rights.

~ Around the World ~

The polecat does not smell his own stink.

(Xhosa: *Iqaqa aliziva kunuka*.) People are blind to their own defects.

A thief has a burning hat.

(Russian) It means that a criminal will be betrayed by his guilty conscience. (For a thorough Russian literary exploration of this theme, read Dostoevsky's *Crime and Punishment*.)

~ 18 ~

Alcohol

Drink like a fish.

When someone drinks alcohol to excess. We've used this phrase
in English for more than five centuries, before we knew much
about science. You see, fish don't drink water, they breathe
it. The Portuguese say they drink "like a sponge" (*beber como
uma esponja*). Japanese drink "like a python." In France a heavy
imbiber is said "to drink like a hole" (*boire comme un trou*).

On/off the wagon.

A person who abstains from alcohol (usually because they had
a problem with it) is said to be "on the wagon," and an alcoholic
who starts drinking again after an attempt at sobriety "is off
the wagon." So what is this wagon? Back in the day, the saying
was "on the water wagon." As horse-drawn water wagons
disappeared, so did the first part of the phrase. The idea was that
the person on the wagon was drinking water instead of wine.

Three sheets to the wind.

Drunk. This comes from the days of sailing ships. When sailors wanted to refer to someone who was literally groggy (from drinking too much grog), they looked up to the sheets. The sheets were not the sails but the ropes that were attached to the bottom corner of the sails. If they were loose, the sail would flutter around and the ship would veer off course. Sailors saw a certain similarity between a tipsy shipmate and a sail that had gone to the wind. One sheet to the wind was bad enough, but if three of the sheets went, you would be completely out of control.

~ Around the World ~

To look too deeply into the glass.

(German: *Zu tief ins Glas shauen*.) To drink too much. Not to be confused with the phrase "beer goggles," which in English slang means the effect of alcohol on the relative attractiveness of that person you met at the bar at closing time.

There is no standing on one leg.

(German: *Auf einem Bein steht man nicht gut*.) You need at least two drinks to have a good time.

To ride a green horse.

(Indonesian: *Naik kuda hijan*.) To be dead drunk.

A drunkard's purse is a bottle.

(Azerbaijani) Excessive drink leaves you with no money.

~ 19 ~
Gossip

The walls have ears.

Be careful what you say, as you never know who may be listening. We borrowed this phrase, urging discretion, from the Romance languages. Its first appearance in English, according to the *Oxford English Dictionary*, was in 1592 when it appeared as a literal translation of the French (*les murailles ont des aureilles*). Other earlier uses of it come from the Spanish from T. Shelton's 1620 translation of Cervantes's *Don Quixote*. But it is not an exclusively European thought. Taiwanese, Japanese, and Chinese all have variants of the saying. The Korean version is "Talks in day time are heard by birds and at night by mice."

Loose lips sink ships.

Don't reveal others' secrets. It began as a U.S. World War II poster campaign. The purpose was to keep citizens from accidentally revealing the movements of troops or ships in their letters or conversation. The British versions of the slogan were

"Careless talk costs lives" and "Be like dad, keep mum!" Because of its rhyme scheme, the "loose lips" slogan was remembered and passed on to a generation too young to remember the war.

AWKWARD!

Have you ever walked into a room at the most awkward moment possible? For example, you come in carrying a wrapped casserole just as your host is shouting at her husband, "How could you sleep with her?" Or you come into the copy room just in time to hear your boss discussing who is going to be fired. In French they have an expression for that: "To arrive like a hair in the soup" (*Arriver comme un cheveu sur la soupe*).

Speak of the devil.

A short version of the phrase "speak of the devil and he will appear." Said when the person you've just been speaking about walks into the room. In olden days there was a superstition that one should not speak of the devil or one might summon him. Being amused when the very person you were discussing happens to show up is a universal phenomenon. Arabic speakers say, "We mentioned the cat, and it came bounding."

> **WHAT DID YOU JUST SAY?**
>
> Icelandic has the expression "I won't sell it more expensive than I bought it" (*Ég sel það ekki dýrara en keypti það*). Does this mean:
>
> **A.** I am about to share some gossip.
> **B.** This is a gift.
> **C.** I am trying to be well mannered.
> **D.** A penny saved is a penny earned.

ANSWER: A. It is said to relieve the speaker of the consequences of the gossip. "This is what I heard, take it for what it's worth."

~ *Around the World* ~

A fly is resting on a flyswatter.
(Akan) You say this in Ghana to hush someone up when you see that someone you've been gossiping about is approaching.

He ate a wooden wedge.
(Arabic) Someone slandered him.

To eviscerate a cow.
(Argentine Spanish) To bad-mouth someone.

I believe my pig whistles.
(German) If a German person gives you some tasty gossip, you might reply, "*Ich glaub, mein Schwein pfeift*." Literally it means "I believe my pig whistles." What it really means is "I don't believe it!"

~ 20 ~

Laziness

Bump on a log.

There is really only one context in which this phrase appears. "Are you going to just sit there like a bump on a log, or are you going to get up and do something?" This simile was first recorded in American writer Kate Douglas Wiggins's *The Bird's Christmas Carol* in 1899. Even though there are a lot of motionless things in the world, this particular comparison struck a chord and the expression stuck. Both Chinese and English speakers use the term "lazybones" to describe someone sitting like a bump on a log. The Chinese also use the charming expression "lazy bug."

On autopilot.

Going through a task by rote without focus. The autopilot is a mechanical device that keeps a plane flying straight while the pilot does something else. Here's a quiz for you: In what year was the autopilot invented? A. 1980 B. 1973 C. 1926. D. 1914.

Believe it or not, it was 1914. Only eleven years after the Wright Brothers made their first flight, Lawrence Burst Sperry unveiled a device to keep a biplane flying straight and level along the Seine at an aviation safety conference in Paris in June 1914.

CALL THE CAREER COUNSELOR
You know that person at your office who is totally unsuited for his job? In Iceland there is an expression for that: "He's on the wrong shelf in life" (*Hann er á rangri hillu í lífinu*).

~ *Around the World* ~

On with the butter.
(Icelandic: *Áfram með smjörið.*) Stop goofing around and do what you're supposed to be doing.

A wife farming with her husband cannot be lazy.
(Luganda: *Alima ne bba—taba munafu.*) It means that with the support of someone who loves you, you can't be lazy and you cannot fail.

RUSSIAN FUN FACT!

The Russian word for a week (*nedelya*) is derived from the phrase "to do nothing" and originally meant a period of rest. That's a lot of rest!

He who yawns catches not a fish.

(Maori: *Ki te hamama popora te tangata e kore e mau te ikaa.*) Said of someone who starts a job but does not finish it.

You can't catch a louse with one finger.

(Malagasy: *Tondro tokana tsy mahazo hao.*) Success requires effort.

Work in which one just scoots about on the buttocks.

(Navajo: *Naanish t'óó yii' nahaltsaad.*) The Navajo don't have a lot of respect for the kind of work performed while seated in a swivel chair. A cushy job. (See "Nice work if you can get it," p. 142.)

~ 21 ~
Envy

The grass is always greener on the other side of the fence.

It is human nature to believe that what you have is inferior to what the other guy has. You water your lawn but imagine your neighbor's is greener than yours. Japanese speakers envy their neighbor's garden. "The flower of the neighbor is red." Koreans are hungry. "The other person's cake looks larger." And in Taiwan they covet the neighbor's wife. "Other people's wives look more beautiful."

Green-eyed monster.

The color green has been associated with jealousy since the sixteenth century. Etymologists suggest that jade may have something to do with it, but they're not sure why exactly. The phrase "green-eyed monster" itself was one of William Shakespeare's many coinages. It comes from *Othello* in which Iago says: "O, beware my lord, of jealousy. It is the

green-eyed monster which doth mock the meat it feeds on."
Shakespeare wrote of "green-eyed jealousy" before that in
The Merchant of Venice.

**The more milk and banana you give to a snake,
the worse the poison will get.**
(Bengali) If you treat a jealous person well, they will only
become more jealous.

Everyone stones the tree that bears fruit.
(Mexican Spanish: *Al árbol que da frutos, tot el mundo lo
apedrea.*) It is a good sign if people envy you.

Envy sees the sea but not the rocks.
(Russian) It's much easier to envy the movie star giving an
Oscar speech than it is to envy the challenges the actor had to
overcome to get there.

~22~
Cheating

Caught red-handed.

Caught in the act. An allusion to hands stained red by the blood of a murder victim. It began as a Scottish expression but went further afield after Sir Walter Scott used it in his 1819 novel *Ivanhoe*: "I did but tie one fellow, who was taken red-handed and in the fact, to the horns of a wild stag." In Arabic they say, "You stole the cockerel, the feather is on your head."

Sold a bill of goods.

Swindled. There is nothing nefarious about selling someone a bill of goods in the literal sense. A bill of goods is simply a list of the things that will be provided. Trouble comes only when someone takes money for a list of goods and then disappears before providing them. There have been enough crooked salesmen throughout history for the term to refer almost exclusively to a con.

~ Around the World ~

The turtle's feet slowly appear.

(Taiwanese) The truth (usually a nefarious one) is revealed. The mask slips.

Don't let your daughter-in-law eat your autumn eggplants.

(Japanese) Don't let anyone take advantage of you.

To go looking for wool and come back shorn.

(Spanish: *Fue por lana y salió trasquilado.*) Intending to cheat someone and being cheated yourself instead.

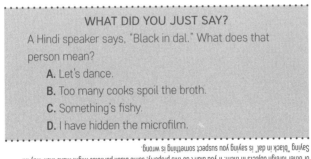

WHAT DID YOU JUST SAY?

A Hindi speaker says, "Black in dal." What does that person mean?

    A. Let's dance.

    B. Too many cooks spoil the broth.

    C. Something's fishy.

    D. I have hidden the microfilm.

ANSWER: C. When you make dal from scratch, you need to sift the lentils to make sure there are no little stones or other foreign objects in them. If you didn't do this properly, some black particles might make their way in. Saying "black in dal" is saying you suspect something is wrong.

~ 23 ~

Lies

Pull the wool over one's eyes.

To deceive. Etymologists have come up with all sorts of
colorful theories as to the origin of this saying, most of
them pure fancy. What they agree on is that the "wool" is a
reference to a wig from the days when the upper classes wore
powdered wigs. Pulling a wig over someone's eyes would
temporarily blind him so you could do something while he
wasn't looking. A Xhosa equivalent is "You've rubbed tobacco
into my eyes" (*Wandidyobh' intshongo emehlweni*). Between
the two, I would go with the wool.

Economical with the truth.

Said of a liar. The cliché sounded original back in the mid-1980s
when British Cabinet Secretary Sir Robert Armstrong used it
to describe Peter Wright's book *Spycatcher* in the Supreme
Court of Wales. That is when people started to repeat it in
large numbers, but Armstrong might have read Mark Twain

who wrote, "Truth is a valuable commodity, and we have to be economical with it."

Urban myth/legend.

A story with a modern setting that seems plausible but is entirely made up or embellished, especially the types of stories that get passed along through word of mouth and people's social media feeds without any fact-checking. "Urban legend" is the older of the two expressions. An example can be found in the *New York Times* in 1925: "Around the subject of population there has been a growth of popular legend hard to remove. Great Britain illustrates the urban legend." The phrase "urban legend" is getting a bit shopworn. I would like to propose adopting the Dutch term "a monkey-sandwich story" (*een broodje aap verhal*).

~ *Around the World* ~

Goats fall that take hold of lichens.

(Kikuyu: *Ciĩgwatagĩrĩa mareru.*) Lichens are not strong enough to hold a falling goat. The saying is a response to an unsatisfactory excuse. "Likely story."

Throwing cream into one's eyes.

(Croatian: *Bacati kajmak u oči.*) It is what you say of someone who is obviously lying.

Pay the duck.

(Portuguese: *Pagar o pato*.) To take the blame for something you did not do.

To sell donuts.

(Romanian: *Vinde gogoși*.) To lie.

To not put clothes on one's teeth.

(Japanese) To tell it like it is.

24

Fraud & Crime

Crime doesn't pay.

Etymologists have unearthed examples of writers using the line "crime doesn't pay" as early as 1892, but it did not become a fixed phrase until the 1930s when it was spoken by The Shadow at the end of each broadcast of the radio drama. "The weed of crime bears bitter fruit . . . crime does not pay . . . the Shadow knows (laugh)." It became an FBI slogan in the 1950s and then a catchphrase for the cartoon detective Dick Tracy. But is it true? Not everyone thinks so. Kikuyu has a proverb that suggests bad guys do prosper: "The forest of an unpleasant person is the one that has trees" (*Gatiũ ka mũimwo nĩ irĩ noko karĩ mĩtĩ*).

Plead the Fifth.

Not admitting to a crime or misdeed. It is often used outside its strictly legal context. "Did you eat the last cookie?" "I plead the Fifth." Thanks to American television, I am reliably informed that the phrase is also occasionally used in the U.K. even though it is a reference to the U.S. Constitution. (In fact, I was once asked by a British friend, "What is the Fifth, anyway?") The Fifth Amendment reads in part, "No person . . . shall be compelled in any criminal case to be a witness against himself." The same amendment spells out the right to a trial by jury and the prohibition of "double jeopardy" (being tried twice for the same offense), and says that private property shall not be taken for public use without due process of the law.

C'EST WHAT?!

ITS NAME IS PETER, AND IT COMES BACK (*SI CHIAMA PIETRO E TORNA INDIETRO*).

You ask your Italian friend if you can borrow a copy of this book. She replies, "Yes, but its name is Peter." Before you respond, "Okay, can I borrow a copy of Peter, then?" you should know that this is the first part of an idiom so common that people use it in an abbreviated form. The full version is "Its name is Peter, and it comes back" (*Si chiama Pietro e torna indietro*). This is still a weird way to ask for an object's return, but it has a nice rhyme in Italian, and so it stuck. In any case, give the book back when you're done reading it.

Cook the books.

Accounting ledgers with a dash of Tabasco. Yum. Cooking the books means organizing the financial results in such a way as to make things seem rosier than they are. Another way of saying this is "creative accounting." The idea here is that something has been "cooked up." Conjured. Scottish poet Tobias Smollett's 1751 *The Adventures of Peregrine Pickle* offers an early example: "Some falsified printed accounts, artfully cooked up, on purpose to mislead and deceive."

An eggplant on a plate.

(Hindi) Eggplants are round, so they roll around a plate just like the shifting loyalties of one who cannot be trusted.

There is no cunning person whoever licked himself on the back.

(Zulu: *Akukho qili lazikhotha emhlane.*) Said of a foolish criminal whose half-baked scheme went pear-shaped.

~ 25 ~

Patience

Don't count your chickens before they're hatched.

This saying, which means not to celebrate prematurely, was the moral of one of Aesop's fables, and versions of it are used throughout the Western world. In a number of Romance languages, including French, Italian, Spanish, Portuguese, and Romanian, you are similarly warned not to sell the bear's skin before you've caught him. Arab speakers say, "It's like selling fish still in the sea."

Go off half-cocked.

It's a musket reference. Muskets were not always reliable, and sometimes when the hammer was cocked halfway, a faulty firing mechanism would cause it to shoot before it was supposed to. This happened often enough to be used metaphorically whenever someone was too anxious and acted before they were prepared. "Jump the gun" has a similar meaning. It is a reference to the starting pistol at a race. When a runner takes off before the signal, she jumps the gun. Russians say such a person goes "galloping across Europe." Xhosa speakers say, "The swallow has anticipated summer" (*Inkonjane iliphangele ihlobo*).

Around the World

The devil dictates when you hurry.

(Polish: *Co nagle, to po diable.*) A 1973 study at Princeton University supports this old proverb. In the experiment, forty theology students were asked to prepare a small talk and to go to another building to deliver it. Half were asked to speak on a nonreligious topic, the other half on the parable of the Good Samaritan, which highlights the virtue of helping those in need. The experimenters told some of the students that they were late for their talk and told other students that they had plenty of time. As they walked to the next building, they passed someone lying on the ground. The researchers found that those who had been thinking about the Good Samaritan were no more likely to help than those who had not. The main factor that determined whether or not a student stopped to help was how much of a hurry the student thought he/she was in. Those who were rushed did not stop, while those who had time did.

Not crossing the ice after one night of frost.

(Dutch: *Niet over één nacht ijs gaan*.) Don't do something rash. Have patience.

Hurry, hurry has no blessing.

(Swahili: *Haraka haraka haina baraka*.) Haste makes waste. It doesn't sound like much in its English translation, but look at what a great little rhyme it is in Swahili.

The cow comes only after the cowbell.

(Basque: *Behia baino lechen zintzarria*.) Wait for it!

~ 26 ~

Perseverance

What doesn't kill you makes you stronger.

If someone accuses you of reading too much self-help after you say this, you can respond, "Au contraire, my friend. I am quoting Nietzsche." Tell her you have been reading his 1889 essay "Twilight of the Idols." You can also mention that the philosopher was inspired by an earlier work, *Maxims of Hyperborean,* which said, "What does not destroy us, we destroy and it makes us stronger." Feign ignorance of the Kelly Clarkson song. In Otjiherero they say, "What doesn't kill you makes you fat." I can attest to that.

Keep a stiff upper lip.

Because the lip starts to tremble when a person cries, this phrase, associated with the British, means not to show one's emotion, especially when one is distressed. The British have a companion saying urging their peers to maintain a sunny disposition in the face of trouble, "Keep your pecker up." This is not referring to what Americans might assume. The pecker here is a bird's beak.

~ Around the World ~

Put up with it, Cossak, you'll get to be the head of your tribe.

(Russian) Analogous to the English "No pain, no gain."

Three day monk.

(Japanese) A quitter. This would also be a good rock band name.

Dying and rising as the moon does.

(Xhosa: *Umaf' evuka, nje ngenyanga*.) This refers to a tenacious person who has been beaten down many times and gotten back up again. (Cue the Chumbawamba song . . .)

~ 27 ~
Appreciation

Casting pearls before swine.

This expression for effort wasted on those who can't appreciate or benefit from it is from the Sermon on the Mount in the New Testament (Matthew 7:6). The image of throwing jewels in front of a pig captured the collective imagination a bit more than the first part of the verse: "Give not that which is holy unto the dogs." But you don't have to be Christian to appreciate that kind of futility. The Korean language has "Chanting Buddhist sutra to a cow's ear." The Japanese language has "Chanting prayer to a horse's ear." In Chinese they are "playing a musical instrument to a cow," and in Thai they are "playing the violin for the buffalo to listen to." A Kikuyu proverb goes "One does not give any beer to a foolish visitor" (*Mūgeni kīrimū ndarugagīrwo njohi*). In Persian they say, "Not every ass is worthy of saffron."

Don't bite the hand that feeds you.
Don't be ungrateful. The expression has been in use since the 1700s. An early print example was found in Joseph Addison's *The Spectator* (1711): "He is so wonderfully unlucky, insomuch that he will bite the Hand that feeds him." The Chinese version is "to forget favors and betray justice." They also say "catch fish, forget trap," a reference to celebrating a victory while ignoring what made it possible.

NOT KNOWING THE GOOD INTENTION OF THE VISITOR, THE DOG BITES MR. LU

As the Chinese proverb above attests, people throughout the world have had the experience of doing a good deed only to be repaid with resentment or abuse. The English equivalent of this thought might be "No good deed goes unpunished." In Japan and Korea they speak of "treating someone with sake and getting slapped in the face."

~ 28 ~
Responsibility

God helps those who help themselves.
About three-quarters of Americans believe this self-reliance proverb is a Bible verse. It is not. Those who know it is not biblical say it comes from Benjamin Franklin's *Poor Richard's Almanac*. They're wrong, too. It came from English politician Algernon Sydney in his 1698 article "Discourses Concerning Government." But then again, that's not entirely right either, because way before Sydney, the ancient Greek slave and storyteller Aesop wrote, "The gods help them who help themselves."

Pull yourself up by your own bootstraps.
Take action to improve your own standing. Commonly said by one who believes himself to be a self-made man to someone who he feels needs to take more responsibility. In its literal form, it is impossible, of course. You can't lift your body by tugging at your own shoes. It may help to know that bootstraps

are those heavy loops you find on the backs of work boots that are used to pull the heavy boot over the ankle. The phrase is invoking the image of putting your boots on and getting to work. Its origins are unknown, but one of the first printed appearances of "bootstrap" in this sense, albeit without "pulling himself up by," was in Irish author James Joyce's masterwork, *Ulysses.* "There were . . . others who had forced their way to the top from the lowest rung by the aid of their bootstraps."

Hold (down) the fort.

Said when leaving a place to the person who will be in charge while the first person is out. An old reference to military fortresses. The idea of holding a fort against an enemy is as old as, well, forts. Somehow the word "down" slipped into the American version of this expression, as if the fort itself were going to float away.

— *Around the World* —

Every sheep is hung by its own leg.

(Turkish: *Her koyun kendi bacağından asılır.*) Each person is responsible for her own actions.

No elephant is overburdened by its own trunk.

(Xhosa: *Akukho ndovu isindwa ngumboko wayo.*) Each person should bear his own responsibilities.

You are responsible for plucking your nose hair.

(Luganda: *Olwoya lwomunnyindo—olweggya wekka.*) Nobody else is going to do it for you.

WHAT DID YOU JUST SAY?

You start to tell your Samoan coworker about a problem you are having with a client. She says, "Coral blocks have nothing to do with the preparation of masi" (*E le aia puga I le masi*). What does that mean?

    A. Be patient and a solution will come to you.

    B. This is no concern of mine.

    C. You do not need to spend money to solve this problem.

    D. You are in the wrong job.

ANSWER: B. Your coworker is saying it is not her problem. She is the coral block in this metaphor, and masi is a fermented breadfruit. One has nothing to do with the other.

~ 29 ~
Flexibility

Roll with the punches.

To adapt to the situation. A bit of boxing jargon. When a skilled boxer is punched, he rolls with it by moving his body in such a way that it will not be as punishing. An early example in a boxing context comes from the *Boston Globe* in 1903: "He repeated the blow a few seconds later. . . . Johnson allowed his head to roll with the punches and was not hurt." It was but a short leap from here to the notion of rolling with emotional blows. The Japanese convey the need to adapt to circumstances by saying, "Life is like Old Sai's horse." It alludes to an old folktale about an old man whose horse ran away. His neighbors came to console him, but he told them not to worry, and eventually the horse came back in the company of a faster horse. His neighbors congratulated him, but he told them not to celebrate, and soon thereafter the man's son was riding the fast horse and fell off, breaking his leg. The story goes on like this with fortune and misfortune changing places. The moral is that you don't really know what life will throw at you. What seems like fortune may be misfortune in disguise and vice versa.

Keep calm and carry on.

The slogan comes from posters created by the British government during World War II. They were designed to be posted in areas that were the targets of German bombing raids. The message is self-explanatory. The thing is, the Brits decided not to post them and they were not popularized until one of the few that had not been destroyed was discovered and put up in a used-book shop. Customers wanted to know where they could get one of their own. Today the answer is just about anywhere.

～ Around the World ～

A dog, yes, even a goat, yes, but who ever heard of a sheep sitting on a chair?

(Yoruba) You can be flexible only up to a point.

~ 30 ~

Focus

To have one's head in the clouds.

To be an unrealistic daydreamer. The first recorded instance of people floating around in this manner was in British author Maria Edgeworth's 1806 novel *Leonora*. The metaphor of floating seems to come naturally to people, as similar phrases exist around the world. The Italian phrase is much like our own: "To live in the clouds" (*Vivere nelle nuvole*). The Russians also say, "To float in the clouds." The French go all the way to outerspace with "always on the moon" (*toujours dans la lune*). Both Spanish and Navajo speakers, interestingly, turn to dance metaphors. For the Spanish it is "to be dancing in Bethlehem" (*bailando en Belén*), and for the Navajo it is "dancing too long, he/she keeps absently dancing away."

Red herring.

A red herring is a type of kipper that is smoked until it is partially cooked, allowing it to be stored for a long period of time.

Metaphorically, it is something that distracts from the main issue. But what has that got to do with an old fish? It all started in the pages of English journalist William Cobbett's *Weekly Political Register*. Cobbett, in 1807, wanted to make the point that a false story about a supposed surrender of Napoleon had distracted the press so much that it had completely neglected real matters of importance. He illustrated his thesis with a parable about a young boy who used a red herring to throw the hounds off the scent in a rabbit hunt.

Keep your eye on the ball.

A sports metaphor meaning to maintain focus. It comes from either baseball or the somewhat similar English game rounders. English novelist William Kingston was talking about rounders when he wrote in 1864: "Ellis seized the bat with a convulsive clutch. . . . Remembering Ernest's advice, he kept his eye on the ball and hit it so fairly that he sent it flying away to a considerable distance." The phrase is a bit confounding for non-native speakers, but then they are happy to return the favor. What do you suppose "your eyes fourteen" means? It is a Greek expression that translates "keep your eyes open."

C'EST WHAT?!

THERE ARE ELDERBERRIES IN THE KITCHEN GARDEN, AND YOUR UNCLE IS IN KIEV.

This sounds like a Cold War spy code phrase, but in fact it is a common Russian idiom. It is used to say two things are incompatible or when someone has made a logical connection in conversation that makes no sense. It is sometimes listed as being equivalent to "comparing apples and oranges" and occasionally with the phrase "red herring," but it is not directly equivalent to either. The saying nearly led to an international incident when a Soviet delegate used it at an international conference. His simultaneous translator did not know what an elderberry was and had never heard the expression. Perplexed, but with no time to think, the interpreter improvised and rendered it with the Shakespearean "Something is rotten in the state of Denmark." Everything was fine until the Soviet delegate ended his speech only to be addressed by an angry Danish delegate who rose to protest the "unwarranted slur" on his country and lecture him on the greatness of Denmark compared to "the inhuman, totalitarian system" in the Soviet Union. The confused Soviet, who had never mentioned Denmark, stood to protest the Danish "provocation." A nuclear attack on Denmark was averted when the embarrassed translator confessed to the faux pas.

～ Around the World ～

To live on a cloud made of farts.
(Argentine Spanish: *Vivir en nube de pedos*.) To be out of touch with reality.

To think of blue almonds.
(Polish: *Myśleć o niebieskich migdałach*.) To daydream.

~31~

Conflict

Last straw.

The "last straw" is the final hardship that makes a burden unbearable. The expression itself is an allusion to the longer "the straw that broke the camel's back." In this form it has a biblical sound to it, as Europeans spend little time discussing camels. Although the Bible has a lot to say about camels, there is no parable that matches this saying. *The Oxford Dictionary of Quotations* says it dates to the mid-seventeenth century, but offers no more information than that.

Below the belt. (Also a low blow.)

An unfair attack. This sporting metaphor comes from boxing when, in 1865, the Marquess of Queensberry laid down the rules forbidding punches that landed in that area below the belt. The phrase usually refers to a verbal comment that makes the hearer wince as one might when seeing a boxer punched in this vulnerable region.

FALSE FRIENDS

In English a person swells with pride. If that pride becomes excessive, he might get a swollen head or become too big for his britches. When a French person says, "You are making me swell" (*Tu me gonfles*), he is not feeling pride but anger and indignation. It is similar to "How dare you!"

Bane of my existence.

When was the last time you used the word "bane" outside of this phrase? (Or, for that matter, the word "smithereens" without "blown to"?) When you use this canned expression, you are literally saying your nemesis is poisonous, as it derives from an Old English word for a murderer. It was used in such now-archaic terms as "ratsbane" and "fleabane," which are respectively "rat poison" and "bug poison."

Take someone to the cleaners.

You are not doing anyone's laundry. Rather, you are completely defeating him, usually by wiping him out financially: for example, trying to get a huge settlement in a divorce in order to punish a philandering spouse. "Taken to the cleaners" was once a humorous modernization of the phrase "to be cleaned out." In Iceland they take their adversary to the bakery (*ég tók hann í bakaríið*).

~ *Around the World* ~

Sharp vinegar damages its container.
(Turkish: *Keskin sirke küpüne zarar*.) It means "calm down before you hurt yourself." Dare I say, check yourself before you wreck yourself.

To fight like a belly-up cat.
(Spanish: *Luchar como gato panza arriba*.) No explanation should be necessary if you visualize this for a few seconds.

You can sharpen an ax on the top of his head.
(Russian) Different from the American blockhead, this means someone is very stubborn.

I will find you at the beach!
(Icelandic: *Ég mun finna þig í fjöru*.) I will have my revenge, implying that it will come when you least expect it, for example, while relaxing on the beach.

~ 32 ~
Adversity

Raining cats and dogs.

Heavy rain. This phrase has been with us since the 1600s, and word-watchers have come up with all sorts of creative stories about its origin (the most popular posit that cats and dogs would sleep in the thatched roofs of houses and would fall from their lofts in heavy rain), but the fact is no one really knows why "cats and dogs." It is entirely possible that it has nothing to do with cats or dogs at all and that the human imagination naturally comes up with something large and slightly comical to express heavy rain. Otherwise, how can you explain the Afrikaans "It's raining old women with clubs" (*Ou vrouens met knopkieries reen*), the Faroese "It's raining pilot whales" (*Tað regnar av grind*), the Danish "It's raining cobbler boys" (*Det regner skomagerdrenge*), the Norwegian "It's raining witches" (*Det regner trollkjerringer*), or the Slovak "Tractors are falling" (*Padajú traktory*).

WHO LOVES ADVERSITY?

The people of Sri Lanka, at least if their proverbs are to be believed. There is a Sinhalese saying: "Sweet cakes are bitter, but sweet are misfortunes." It means that hardship is preferable to prosperity. The idea is that the bittersweet cake that is a pleasurable luxury to a poor person is something unpleasant for someone who can afford whatever he wants. In Tamil, another language of Sri Lanka, they say, "In adversity, a fan is a luxury; in time of prosperity, furniture made of ebony and teak becomes a necessity."

In a pickle/jam.

When we want to say we're in a bit of trouble, we turn to these food metaphors. In the United States we most often use "pickle" to refer to pickled cucumbers. In England it often refers to what we'd call pickle relish. So, like jam, it is chopped up and stewing in its juices. Once a fruit or vegetable is in a pickle or a jam, it is unlikely to get back to its original state. "In a pickle" should not be confused with the Dutch phrase "to sit in a pickle" (*in de pekel zitten*). This means you're drunk.

Out of the frying pan and into the fire.

Moving from a bad situation to a worse one. This is a universal experience. In Greek: "Out of the smoke and into the flame." Italian and Portuguese: "Out of the frying pan, into the coals."

Thai: "To escape from the tiger to the crocodile." Hindi: "Fallen from the sky, stuck on a date palm."

When it rains, it pours.

Similar to "out of the frying pan," it means that when bad things happen, they come in a deluge. Occasionally people use it for positive things—usually things that are a bit overwhelming. For example, "I got a promotion. I was invited to speak at a commencement ceremony, and I have a big client coming in for a meeting. When it rains, it pours." The expression, as we use it today, was created by advertising copywriters for Morton Salt. Morton had just added an agent to their product that kept it from getting caked up, so it flowed freely even when it was humid. Someone thought of the old proverb "It never rains, but it pours," and the copywriters adapted it for their purposes. A tremendously successful advertising campaign, indeed. Xhosa speakers refer to someone who has gone through a lot of hardship and survived by saying, "She who has often been rained upon."

～ Around the World ～

If you spit downwards, it hits the beard. If you spit upwards, it hits the mustache.

(Turkish) This is a no-win situation. Six of one, half dozen of the other.

No one becomes a bishop without a beating.

(Icelandic: *Enginn verður óbarinn biskup.*) There are always obstacles to be overcome between a person and his goals.

WHAT DID YOU JUST SAY?

In Ibibio they say, "Do not allow a hunted animal to escape" (*Utuke unam aka ama yak ebat ikpa*). Does this mean:

    A. You've only made him angry.

    B. Easy come, easy go.

    C. Make the best of a bad situation.

    D. Finish what you've started.

ANSWER: C. If you wound an animal and it gets away, you've wasted the effort you put in. So the saying means you should do whatever is necessary to minimize your loss.

C'EST WHAT?!

WHAT IS HIDDEN UNDER THE ANUS WILL BE SEEN BY THE PANT.

You probably think this Ibibio expression means that dirty secrets can never remain entirely hidden. In fact, according to Anietie Akpabio's *Ibibio Proverbs and Idioms*, it means "what a man can do another man can also do. It implies competition by two opponents." I hope that makes it clear.

~ 33 ~
Danger

By the skin of the teeth.

Teeth don't have skin. So where did this way of expressing a close call or near miss come into being? It is from the Geneva Bible, a 1560 translation. Specifically, it comes from the Book of Job, where Job's statement that he had barely escaped with his life was rendered as "I have escaped with the skinne of my teethe." (It's Job 19:20 if you'd like to look it up.) This was a change from a 1535 translation by Miles Coverdale that says "Only there is left me the skin about my teeth," which makes more sense. The King James Bible, which had such an enduring impact on our language, retained the Geneva Bible's wording.

Houston, we have a problem.

Something's wrong. A real astronaut quote from a life-threatening emergency, now used in non-space flight situations, usually in a tongue-in-cheek way. (See "tongue-in-cheek,"

p. 197.) When the ill-fated Apollo 13 moon mission was made the subject of a Hollywood film, director Ron Howard needed to condense several mission control teams into one and make astronaut jargon like "We have a main bus B undervolt" sound riveting to an audience. He also tweaked one particular line of dialogue when the team called down to mission control in Houston to report a major technical fault in the electrical system of one of the service module's oxygen tanks:

> John Swigert: Okay, Houston, we've had a problem here.
> Houston: This is Houston. Say again please.
> Jim Lovell: Houston, we've had a problem. We've had a main B bus undervolt.

This became the on going "Houston, we have a problem." Incidentally, the jargon-filled film was a nightmare for translators. How on earth could they be expected to have an accurate foreign translation for dialogue like: "Talkback is barber poled . . . SM RCS ISOL valves are all gray." Yisrael Yerushalmi, a Hebrew subtitle writer, told the *Jerusalem Post*, "It was horrible, horrible work."

~ Around the World ~

Like a fish on a cutting board.

(Vietnamese) In a very bad situation. A sitting duck.

I caught a lion's tongue.

(Otjiherero: *Mba kambura ongeyama eraka.*) It's a cool trick, but what happens when you let go? This is what someone says when he is in real trouble.

Get the cow off the ice.

(German: *Die Kuh vom Eis holen.*) To escape a dangerous situation.

A hundredweight hanging from a single hair.

(Chinese) The sword of Damocles hanging over your head.

WHAT DID YOU JUST SAY?

In Xhosa there is an expression "You are turning up a mess of red ants" (*Uzinqikel' ubuxhwangu*). What is the best English equivalent?

A. That's a fine kettle of fish!

B. You've opened a can of worms.

C. Beggars can't be choosers.

D. The best thing since sliced bread.

ANSWER: B. It is said of someone who made a statement best left unsaid and stirred up something that can't easily be contained.

~ 34 ~

Risk

Once bitten, twice shy.

The idiom "once bitten, twice shy" has been part of our language since the mid-nineteenth century. But even before that we knew that once a person has had a bad experience, he becomes overly cautious. In the Middle Ages, the English said, "A burnt child dreads the fire." Versions of this proverb appear throughout the world. In southern Nigeria, Ibibio speakers say, "The animal that escapes from a trap is always afraid of something that looks like a trap." Taiwanese and Chinese speakers fear ropes and snakes. The Chinese version of the proverb goes "Once bitten by a snake, one dreads ropes for three years." Japanese speakers, meanwhile, worry about burning their tongues. "Tired of being burnt by hot broth, one blows on a cold dish." The Turkish version of this thought goes "One who has burnt his tongue while drinking milk will blow on yogurt before eating it" (*Sütten ağzı yanan yoğurdu üfleyerek yer*).

To play with fire.

To take an unnecessary risk or tempt fate. If you play with fire, you will probably get burned. The metaphor is old. So old, in fact, that the *Oxford English Dictionary* found an example dating back to around 1325. In Korean they use the expression "pigweed touches the dragon." A little bit of foliage will be no match for a dragon's fire if it tickles his heels too much. Japanese speakers say, "Touch the dragon's beard, step on the tiger's tale." In Chinese they evoke "the praying mantis trying to stop a wagon with its arm" and in Taiwanese "the grasshopper teases the rooster." A grasshopper is one of the rooster's favorite meals.

Around the World

To pat a snake with bare feet.

(Czech: *Hladit hada bosou nohou.*) To do something dangerous. To walk into the metaphorical lion's den.

WHAT DID YOU JUST SAY?

If a Turkish person says, "A sunken fish goes sideways" (*Battı balık yan gider*), does he want you to:

    A. Stop worrying.

    B. Pick up the tab.

    C. Stop beating around the bush.

    D. Invite the family to dinner.

ANSWER: A. When a sunken fish goes sideways, the worst has already happened, so there is no need to keep fretting about it.

~ 35 ~

Mistakes

To bark up the wrong tree.

You're making a mistake, usually referring to a mistaken train of thought. Imagine a hunter going out with a dog at night to hunt raccoons. (He wants to make a nice coonskin cap.) The dog has the animal's scent, and he chases it until it runs up a tree. The hunter knows where to find it because the dog stands at the base of the tree and barks. If, however, he barks up the wrong tree, there will be no raccoon soup for dinner. As you might expect, one of the earliest examples of the phrase in print comes from Davy Crockett. In China they have a much longer view of mistakes and trees as is evident in the proverb "The best time to plant a tree was twenty years ago."

My bad.

My mistake or my fault. This phrasing is almost identical to the old Latin term "mea culpa" (through my own fault). The modern cliché, however, is most often used in a jaunty way when the consequences of an error are not serious. Unlike "I'm sorry," "my bad" assumes forgiveness is unnecessary. The expression seems to have come from the world of sports, specifically professional basketball, and it may have been coined by one NBA player in particular. Manute Bol was a Sudanese immigrant and a native speaker of Dinka. The *St. Louis Post-Dispatch* wrote about Bol on January 10, 1989: "When he throws a bad pass, he'll say, 'My bad,' instead of 'My fault,' and now all the other players say the same thing." And so do we.

Put your foot in your mouth.

A modern version is "open mouth, insert foot." The expression was first recorded in the 1770s about Sir Boyle Roche, who used to say things like "Half the lies our opponents tell about me are not true!" It was derived from the earlier expression "to put one's foot in it" or to make a gaffe, which was probably suggested by someone stepping in dung. The Finns "let a frog out of their mouths" (*päästää sammakko suusta*) when they misspeak. This is not to be confused with the English "having a frog in your throat," which means to be hoarse and refers to the sound of a frog's croak.

~ *Around the World* ~

One cannot live among forty people and never misspeak.
(Yoruba) It is impossible to live in a group and never cause offense.

Even monkeys fall from trees.
(Japanese) Everyone makes mistakes.

~ 36 ~

Overreaction

Tempest in a teapot/teacup.

To make a big fuss over something small. The British prefer the teapot, the Americans the teacup. The saying comes to us from the Latin and first appeared in English as a translation of "*Excitare fluctus in simpulo*" in American lexicographer E. A. Andrews's influential 1854 *Latin Dictionary*. Of course, overreaction is not limited to English speakers, or, for that matter, ancient Romans. In German they "shoot sparrows with cannons" (*mit Kanonen auf Spatzen schießen*), and in Dutch they "shoot a mosquito with a cannon" (*met een kanon op een mug schieten*).

Cut off your nose to spite your face.

Doing something self-destructive believing it will harm your adversary. This vivid image was first recorded in a French text *Historettes* by Gédéon Tallemant des Réaux, written around 1658. "Henry IV well knew that to destroy Paris would be, as they say, to cut off his own nose in taking spite on his own face."

The "as they say" implies that people were using this expression well before this writer dipped his quill. Germans express this sentiment by saying, "Don't cut off the branch you're sitting on" (*Man soll den Ast nicht absägen, auf dem man sitzt*).

INTERNATIONAL OVERREACTIONS

There is action, and then there is overreaction. Just because you have one problem does not mean you should reject everything associated with it. These international phrases express the universal propensity to go a little nuts in the face of adversity.

GERMAN

The Germans were the originators of the now international cliché, "To throw the baby out with the bathwater" (*Das Kind mit dem Bade ausschütten*).

DUTCH

To shoot a mosquito with a cannon. (*Met een kanon op een mug schieten.*)

TURKISH

To burn the duvet because of one flea. (*Pire için yorgan yakmak.*)

~ 37 ~

Blame

Fall guy.

Someone who takes the blame for the misdeed of someone else, or as an individual for the acts of an organization. It is usually used in business or politics. It is an Americanism, but beyond that, scholars throw up their hands and shrug. One theory is that it comes from staged matches in pro-wrestling where someone is chosen to be the winner and another to fall down. A "fall guy," in one word, is a "scapegoat," a term that dates back to biblical times when, as part of the ritual of the Day of Atonement, a pair of goats was chosen to have the sins of the people placed symbolically upon them. The luckier goat was sent out into the wilderness, while its unluckier counterpart was sacrificed. Tyndale's 1530 translation of the Old Testament called the animal that took on people's sins a "scapegoote." The French term is "*bouc émissaire.*" In Spanish you "blame a goat" (*cargarle a una las cabras*) when you accuse someone unjustly.

To throw someone under the bus.

Deflecting blame to someone else to further one's own cause. It is a popular idiom among reality TV contestants. Most word-watchers trace it to a surprising source, a 1984 *Washington Post* article on pop star Cyndi Lauper. "In the rock 'n' roll business, you are either on the bus or under it." How that evolved into someone being pushed under the bus is a bit of a mystery. The Chinese way of expressing a deflection of criticism is "to point to the mulberry tree when the locust tree is to blame."

To pass the buck.

The "buck" here is not a dollar, although no one is entirely sure what it is. What they do know is that the expression came from American poker players in the mid-nineteenth century. Poker players were usually illiterate laborers, and so no one thought to write down their reasoning for posterity. Mark Twain, in 1872, was the first to commit it to paper. In *Roughing It* he says, "I reckon I can't call that hand. Ante and pass the buck." Whatever the "buck" was, it was passed from one player to indicate who would be the next dealer. If someone didn't want to deal, he could pass the buck to the next player. "Passing the buck" became shorthand for giving the responsibility to the next guy in line. President Harry Truman famously had a sign made for his desk that said, "The buck stops here!" Germans also use a gaming metaphor in this situation: "To play off the black Peter to someone" (*Jemandem den schwartzen Peter zuspielen*). Black Peter is a German version of Old Maid. Russians say, "To unload from a sick head to a well one." The Spanish get a bit more dramatic. They say, "To throw the dead body to someone else" (*Echarle el muerto a otro*).

~ *Around the World* ~

Not my circus, not my monkeys.
(Polish: *Nic mój cyrk, nie moje malpy.*) Can we adopt this one, please? It means "not my problem," but it is so much more fun. Let's all start saying this.

~ 38 ~
Insults

Pot calling the kettle black.

Hypocrisy. Both the pot and the kettle are blackened by flame. (Or they were in the days when people cooked over fire.) When pots insult kettles, they exhibit a particular unawareness of their own similar faults. Hypocrisy is not an English invention, of course. Arabic speakers say, "The camel cannot see its own hump." In Kikuyu they say, "The hyena calls another hyena worse than itself" (*Hiti ĩtaga irĩa ĩngĩ ya mũtĩrĩ*). In Taiwan "the turtle laughs at the terrapin that it has no tail, and the terrapin laughs at the turtle that it has rough skin." The Japanese, who are often earthy in their expressions, say that "mucus laughs at snot."

Left-handed compliment.

Something that sounds like a compliment but is actually an insult. It goes back to the marriage practices of German royalty in the Middle Ages, naturally. When a member of the royalty married a commoner, the commoner agreed that she and her children would make no claims on the royal titles or fortunes. All she got was a gift (called a "morning gift") the morning after the marriage was consummated. As it was considered to be a lesser wedding, the groom gave the bride his left hand instead of the traditional right.

Excuse my French.

Nothing at all to do with foreign-language study. Since the late nineteenth century, English speakers have been saying this to apologize for swearing. It derives from an English stereotype of the French as more permissive and bawdy. The French do not say, "Excuse my English." They do, however, sometimes jokingly refer to the English as "roast beefs" as a put-down of their culinary inferiority. (I would have gone with "spotted dick" or "mushy peas," myself.)

WHAT DID YOU JUST SAY?

The French have a saying, "To look at one another like earthenware dogs" (*Se regarder en chiens de faïence*). What does this mean?

A. To look at each other with cold distrust.

B. To flirt.

C. To be married.

D. To be arrogant with one another.

ANSWER: A. The dogs are staring one another down, and they are inanimate.

Sticks and stones may break my bones, but words will never hurt me.

This little ditty is uttered on playgrounds in a singsong fashion by children who are being taunted and who want to pretend they don't care. The *Oxford English Dictionary* states that "sticks and stones" came into being before 1862, because in that year the *Christian Recorder* called it "the old adage." The Papiamento language has its own version without the catchy rhyme. They say, "Swearing does not break bones."

~ Around the World ~

Stop climbing on my head!

(Arabic) Stop annoying me! That would be annoying.

TAKING A LONG WALK ON A SHORT PIER

Every language has a colorful phrase to tell someone to hit the bricks. In Latvian it is "Go pick mushrooms!" (*Ej bekot!*) In Spanish, "Go fry asparagus!" (¡*Manda a freir esparragos!*) In Yiddish, "Grow like an onion with your head in the ground!" Swedish, "Go where the pepper is growing!" (*Dra dit pepparn växer!*) In Navajo it is "Farther on, you coyote!" Italians have one of the kindest ways of telling someone to go jump in a lake: they say, "Go get blessed" (*Vai a farti benedire*).

INTERNATIONAL INSULTS

Tempers flare when people get hungry, and expressing anger through food-related clichés is a global phenomenon.

XHOSA

He is an ash heap's cob. (Ngumpha we zala.)
Compares a person of no character to a cob without grain that has been chucked away into the fire pit.

HINDI

Which farm is that radish from?
A contemptuous phrase for someone trying to act smart.

CHILEAN SPANISH

Look how far the peanut jumped. (Salto lejos el mani.)
If someone in Chile says this to you, they are really telling you that you have no idea what you're talking about and you should mind your own business.

FRENCH

Mind your own onions! (Occupe-toi de tes oignons.)
The French are a bit more pungent when they want you to mind your own business.

ITALIAN

Don't break my chestnuts. (Non mi rompere i maroni.)
This is something you would say to an annoying Italian.

~ 39 ~
Exhaustion &
Frustration

To be at the end of one's rope.

Sometimes "at the end of one's tether." Picture an animal on a tether trying to get to a bowl of food, but he has stretched the cord as far as it will go and the bowl is still just out of reach. That is how you feel when your goal is within sight, but you just do not have the energy or resources to do any more. The earliest uses of the expression said, "Run to the end of his rope," as in the first recorded instance in the *Oxford English Dictionary* written in 1653 by the English poet John Cleveland: "But the Squib is run to the end of the Rope." The Germans evoke the image of someone without the vocabulary to communicate anymore. They say one is "at the end of his Latin" (*mit dem Latein am Ende sein*).

To be at wit's end.

Being at the end of one's rope is to have run out of energy or resources. Being at the end of one's wit means you've run out of ideas. It conveys a feeling of frustration and anxiety. Not knowing how to solve a problem is absolutely driving you crazy. Indonesian and Navajo speakers use practically the same metaphor. Indonesians say, "I have run out of mind" (*kehabisan akal*), and Navajo say, "Thought has run out" (*T'óó bit ninikééz*).

Around the World

Tight like a seppa.
(Japanese) A seppa is a sword mounting. The sword fits in snugly, so it means "stuck."

Legs like curry.
(Gujarati: *Pag nee curry.*) So exhausted that your legs are like a mushy spiced dish.

~ 40 ~

Justice

Hoist by his own petard.

A high-falutin' way to say someone was done in by his own misdeeds. (So high-falutin' you'll find it in Shakespeare's *Hamlet*.) The "petard" was a medieval explosive device that, when set wrong, had a nasty habit of blowing up the person who made it instead of its target. In Samoan, when they want to say someone has been done in by his own actions, they say, "A crab is pierced with his own leg" (*E gase la pa'a I lona vae*).

You reap what you sow.

The bad deeds you put out into the world will come back on you. This is a biblical allusion (see Galatians 6:7). Another version, which dates to the 1970s, is "What goes around comes around," or as John Lennon put it, "Instant karma's gonna get you." In Turkey they express the same sentiment by saying, "One who enters a Turkish bath sweats."

Around the World

The turtle's feet slowly appear.
(Taiwanese) The truth (usually a nefarious one) is revealed. The mask slips.

The one tending the fire is the most likely to be singed.
(Xhosa: *Isikhuni sibuya nomkhwezeli.*) Equivalent to "What goes around comes around."

~41~

Work

Nice work if you can get it.
Usually used in a jokey way about a job that sounds too good to be true for one reason or another. "Would you believe they pay me to sit in empty seats at the Oscars?" "Nice work if you can get it." The phrase was popularized by a tune by American composer George Gershwin written for the Fred Astaire film *A Damsel in Distress*. Germans call this a "bomb job" (*bombenjob*), and that is such a fun word that I think we should, too.

Jack of all trades.
A "jack of all trades" is a dilettante. The full version of the phrase is "a jack of all trades and a master of none." Many people have forgotten the last part, and so it is sometimes used as a positive to refer to someone with a lot of talents. In Korea they say that "one who has twelve kinds of talent has no food for tonight's dinner." There is a similar phrase in Taiwan, but there Jack has only "ten trades" and "no food to eat."

No rest for the wicked.

This adage literally means that the wicked will have no rest because they will be tormented by their consciences. It appears here under "work," however, because these days it is more often used humorously when speaking to someone who is very busy. It comes from the Bible, Isaiah 57, and was traditionally phrased "no peace for the wicked."

~ Around the World ~

To pull the little cart.

(Italian: *Tirare la carretta.*) To slog through all of those little, everyday tasks.

THE ONE-BEAR RULE

"A hungry bear won't dance" (*Aç ayı oynamaz*) goes the Turkish saying. It means that everyone must be paid for their work. This dates back to the days when busking Roma *Usari*, or "bear handlers," roamed Eastern Europe with dancing bears. This was more recent than you might think. According to the friend who shared this idiom with me, "There was a law that only one bear was allowed on a bus when I first went to Turkey in 1981. Two bears might fight on the bus, so it was a strict one-bear rule."

~ 42 ~
Preparation &
Planning

The early bird catches the worm.

The one who gets up or gets started first will get the reward. This is a very old expression dating back to at least 1636 when it appeared in English historian William Camden's *Remaines of a Greater Worke Concerning Britaine*. Germans say, "The morning hour has gold in its mouth" (*Morgenstund hat Gold im Mund*). Japanese: "To wake up early gets you three coins." Ibibio: "The first person to reach the stream in the morning sees its beauty" (*Ebemiso idim ekit enyin idim*).

Close the barn door after the horse has escaped.

Making a plan after the worst has already occurred. The thought, if not the exact wording, is very old. The Dutch scholar Erasmus recorded a similar proverb in his *Adages* in 1536. The Latin version was "help after the war is over" (*post bellum auxiliom*). Earlier English speakers phrased it "to shut the stable door after the steed is stolen," which has a bit more alliteration than the modern version. Other cultures have noticed this tendency as well. Chinese has "the wood is already made into a boat," which is a bit like "that ship has sailed." Korean has "to beat the drum in vain after the event has already ended," and Taiwanese has "the rice has already been cooked," which I am reliably informed is often used when an unwed woman has become pregnant.

A stitch in time saves nine.

When I was young, I thought that time was being stitched. It was poetic, but the saying was incomprehensible to me. Of course, what it really means is that in time, the stitch you make today will keep you from having to do nine more stitches in the future. Put in an effort today to spare yourself a larger effort tomorrow. The English have been expounding this work ethic since at least the 1730s.

WHAT DID YOU JUST SAY?

The French have an expression "to have a fat morning." Does this mean:

A. To be hung over.
B. To sleep in.
C. To eat a big breakfast.
D. To get up on the wrong side of the bed.

ANSWER: B. To have a fat morning is to sleep in.

~ Around the World ~

To push something with your belly.
(Portuguese: *Empurrar com a barriga.*) To keep putting
something off.

Being prepared is not a sign of weakness.
(Luganda: *Okwerinda sibuti.*) The Boy Scouts and Girl Scouts
would agree with this, as it echoes their international motto "Be
prepared."

A plan hatched in the coyote way.
(Navajo) A crazy scheme.

~43~
Leadership

The blind leading the blind.

Applied to inept leaders. This one was coined by Jesus of Nazareth, who was a master of vivid metaphor. It can be found in the New Testament in Matthew 15:14 and Luke 6:39. Because it is biblical, variants exist throughout the Christian world. "If the blind lead the blind, both fall into a ditch" is how the French (*Si un aveugle conduit un autre aveugle, ils tombent tous deux dans le fossé*) and Italians (*Se un cieco guida l'altro, tutti e due cascano nella fossa*) phrase it.

When the cat's away, the mice will play.

Sometimes shortened to "When the cat's away . . ." When the authority figure is not around, people will break the rules. This phenomenon has been observed all over the world, of course. Thai speakers say, "When the cat is not there, the mouse is happy." In Zulu it is "The weasel is at ease because the mamba has gone out" (*Uchakide uhlolile imamba yalukile*). Ibibio has a particularly vivid version: "When the head of the house is away, the person with ulcers goes to the waterpot to drink."

To breathe down someone's neck.

To watch so closely your presence is disruptive; to micromanage. This saying is not very old, dating back only as far as 1946. The *Oxford English Dictionary* records its first use in the novel *Lost Haven* by the Australian writer Kylie Tennant, but her meaning was slightly different: "There were big black moths in the wardrobe; not to mention a beastly big mountain breathing down the back of your neck." The first appearance in print with its current sense was not until 1959 when the *London Times* wrote, "Because Kent were always breathing down their necks, Hampshire could never really establish themselves." The Russian version of this expression is particularly deep. They say that an overly watchful person is "sitting on someone's soul."

Too many cooks spoil the broth.

Cooperation doesn't always make things easier. When too many people are responsible for a project, it is a recipe for conflict, things falling through the cracks and being pulled in too many directions at once (to use a few idioms). There are parallels in many languages. In Persian they say, "Two captains sink the ship." The Russians say, "With seven nurses, the child goes blind." In Italian, "With too many roosters crowing, the sun never comes up," and in Japanese, "Too many boatmen run the boat up the top of the mountain."

AN EXPRESSION WE NEED

When a Swedish politician becomes embroiled in a scandal (anything to which we in the U.S. would add the suffix "-gate"), he goes through a familiar ritual. He admits his wrongdoing. ("I have not lived up to the high standards I set for myself or this office.") Then he promises to do better and asks for forgiveness. The Swedish call this "doing the full poodle." I propose we adopt this phrase. We need it.

~ *Around the World* ~

When two elephants fight, it's the grass that gets hurt.

(Swahili: *Wapiganapo tembo wawili ziumiazo nyasi.*) When the right and powerful clash, the weak and powerless pay the price.

There's no "I" in team.

Members of a team must put the interest of the group above
their own. Generally speaking, the United States is good at
producing clichés about individual achievement. ("Rugged
individualism" and "self-made man" are two good examples of
the kinds of phrases Americans like to invent and bandy about.)
Eastern cultures are more prone to coin and pass on phrases
celebrating cooperation. There are two exceptions, two places
where Americans sing the virtues of the team, and those
are professional sports and business motivational seminars.
"There's no 'I' in team" came out of the former and made its
way to the latter. Business types love sports metaphors. As a
motivational phrase, it has long ago lost its usefulness and has
been relegated to the realm of parody. It is the prime example
of the kind of thing an overly cheery motivational speaker would
say. The phrase seems to have suddenly exploded into public
consciousness in 1965. Why is not clear. There are a couple

of quotes of local sports figures using the expression before October 1965 when baseball pitcher Vernon Law was named comeback player of the year and was quoted saying this in a widely circulated wire story. This may have been what made it go viral. (See "To go viral" p. 228.)

Many hands make light work.

This cliché needs no explanation. I have included this entry primarily so I can say the words "Bevis of Hampton." Although it is not well-known today, Bevis was one of the most popular tales of the medieval period. You could say it was the *Game of Thrones* of the period in which *Game of Thrones* is set. It was from this tale, written by an anonymous author around the year 1330, that you first find this old saw (then a new saw) "Þe Ascopard be strong & sterk, Mani hondes makeþ light werk!" In case you're wondering how to be "sterk," it means hard and unyielding.

Like herding cats.

A nearly impossible organization task, usually referring to a group of people. "Getting everyone to turn in their reports on time is like herding cats." The image needs no explanation to anyone who has spent any time trying to get a cat to do anything. (In case you were wondering, the collective noun for cats is "clowder.") Herding cats was an original notion back in 1986, the first year that the *Oxford English Dictionary* records a reference to it. Not so any longer.

~ *Around the World* ~

The sheep that gets separated from the flock, gets eaten by the wolf.

(Turkish: *Sürüden ayrılanı kurt kapar.*) Used to tell someone to stay with the group.

Many people pick up firewood, the fire flames high.

(Chinese) You build a bigger fire when everyone pitches in.

WHAT DID YOU JUST SAY?

"Three smelly cobblers are better than Zhuge Liang."

This Chinese phrase corresponds to the English:

   A. Better than a poke in the eye with a sharp stick.

   B. Two heads are better than one.

   C. Read between the lines.

   D. A bird in the hand is worth two in the bush.

ANSWER: B. Zhuge Liang was a wise statesman, and the idea here is that it is better to have a group of people, even lowly cobblers, than one genius. A Japanese version of this saying is "When three people get together, you have the wisdom of Manjusri." Manjusri was the bodhisattva of transcendent wisdom, a bodhisattva being someone who has attained enlightenment but compassionately sticks around in the mortal realm, instead of going to nirvana, to teach those who are less enlightened.

~ 45 ~
Sales & Buying

Pig in a poke.

Buying something without knowing in advance what it is. A "poke" is a small bag. When you buy a pig in a sack, you don't know what kind of small animal is wriggling about in there. So the story goes that unscrupulous vendors would put stray cats into sacks and try to pawn them off as pigs. Sometimes the seller looked inside and discovered the con, and this is where the expression "letting the cat out of the bag" comes from. It is hard to imagine that the meowing wouldn't have given the trick away, but there must be something to this, as other languages have versions of the idiom. In German they say "to buy a cat in a sack" (*die Katze im Sack kaufen*), and apparently they say the same in Swedish, Polish, Latvian, and Norwegian. In Indonesian it is "to buy a water buffalo in a field."

Ballpark figure.

An Americanism used in financial negotiations, usually when you're asking for an estimate on the cost of something, but you're not committing the person to an exact figure. A short version of this is simply "ballpark." For example, "How much will it cost to replace the whole roof, ballpark?" This is a reference to the stadium where baseball is played. As long as the ball is hit within the park, as opposed to over the fence, it is in play. So asking for a "ballpark figure" is asking for the outer parameters.

Sell like hotcakes.

Something that is tremendously popular and sells quickly. Hotcakes tend not to do this anymore, but there was a time when they did. At the beginning of the nineteenth century, hotcakes were made of cornmeal and cooked in lard and served piping hot at fairs, sort of like elephant ears at a carnival today. Yum. In Japan they say, "It sold so well it grew wings."

~ *Around the World* ~

Buying something for an apple and an egg.

(Dutch: *Iets voor een appel en een ei kopen*.) Cheaply.

AN ARM AND A LEG

When something is way too expensive, Americans say it costs "an arm and a leg." The French express sticker shock by saying it costs "the eyes in your head" (*coûter les yeux de la tête*). This sounds more disgusting to us than the arm and leg thing only because we're not used to hearing it and therefore imagine it literally. The Spanish "say only pay one eye" (*me costó un ojo de la cara*) or sometimes a liver (*me costó un riñón*).

~ 46 ~
# Money & Wealth

Midas touch.
A literary allusion to the Greek myth of King Midas. Everything Midas touched turned to gold. We usually use this expression to mean someone is especially lucky, forgetting that Midas was a cautionary figure. Midas turned his daughter to a lifeless statue and died of starvation because all of his food turned to metal.

Money makes the world go round.
This phrase touting the importance of money traces its origin to the 1966 musical *Cabaret*. The notion that money is important is, of course, nothing new. In Asia, money is imbued with supernatural power. "Have money," says a Korean phrase, "and you can make devil or God run errands for you." "With money," say both the Japanese and Chinese, "you can make the devil work the mill."

C'EST WHAT?!

THEY SPLASH THE SKYR WHO OWN IT
(ÞEIR SLETTA SKYRINU SEM EIGA ÞAÐ).

To start with, what is "skyr"? Skyr (pronounced "skeer") is an Icelandic delicacy that is like yogurt, but is not yogurt. Don't let an Icelander catch you calling it yogurt. Skyr has been eaten in Iceland since medieval times, but it is starting to find its way into the dairy aisles in the United States as the next big thing after Greek yogurt. It takes three liters of milk to produce one liter of skyr, so for a poor person, it was a luxurious and occasional treat. This means that only a person who can afford skyr can afford to waste it by splashing it around. That is the literal sense, but it is used ironically, so it actually implies that even though the person is wealthy enough to think he can do whatever he wants with his skyr, it actually makes him look like an idiot. Therefore it is often translated with the English proverb "People who live in glass houses shouldn't throw stones."

A penny saved is a penny earned.

Better to be thrifty than to have to go out and earn more money. Usually attributed to Benjamin Franklin, what he actually wrote was "a penny saved is twopence dear," and he was not the first to express this sentiment. George Herbert's *Outlandish Proverbs*, circa 1633, records, "A penny spar'd is twice got."

DO THE GERMANS ENVY THE FRENCH?

How else can you explain the fact that when a German wants to imagine someone who lives like a king, she says *he lives "like God in France"* (wie Gott in Frankreich).

~ Around the World ~

Stretch your feet according to your blanket.

(Turkish: *Ayağını yorganına göre uzat.*) Spend within your means.

Lakshmi abandons the reckless spender.

(Bengali) Lakshmi is the goddess of wealth.

He who doesn't have a dog, hunts with a cat.

(Portuguese: *Quem não tem cão caça com gato.*) Make the most of what you've got.

~47~
Travel

A rolling stone gathers no moss.

A version of this aphorism is found in the *Adages of Erasmus*, a collection of Greek and Latin proverbs first published in 1500. The Greek version was "a rolling stone does not gather seaweed," and the Latin was "a rolling stone is not covered with moss" (*musco lapis volutus haud obducitur*). Today we interpret this as a good thing. Someone who keeps moving does not get bogged down. A Kikuyu version of this is "By staying always in the same place, one gets lice" (*Gĩkaro kĩmwe kĩrĩ ngee kana ndaa*). And the Mongolian language has "A travelling fool is better than a sitting wise person (*Suusan tsetnees yavsan teneg deer*). This was not always how English speakers interpreted the proverb. It originally meant that a person who was always on the move would never build up much money or position, as witnessed by this 1579 version recorded by English satirist Stephen Gosson in his book *Ephemerides of Phialo*: "A rowling stone gathers no mosse, and a running hed wil neuer thriue." Many Asian languages retain this point of view. For example, the Taiwanese say, "A hen that keeps moving its nest lays no eggs," and the Japanese say, "A tree often replanted will not spread its roots."

Across the pond.

A joking and clichéd way to refer to the Atlantic Ocean used on both sides of the pond (i.e., by both British and North American speakers). The phrase is far older than you might think. Early examples of oceanic understatement uncovered by etymologists include "great pond" in 1641 and "herring-pond" in 1686.

Men are like the lip of the cooking pot which forms just one circle.

(Malagasy: *Ny olombelona toy ny molo-bilany, ka iray mihodidina ihany.*) Although people may be different from one another (on different parts of the lip of the pot), they are all part of the same whole (the pot). People are people.

To have your legs stolen.

(Japanese) To be without transportation.

~48~
Greed

A bird in the hand is worth two in the bush.

Don't give up what you have for a dream of something better. This is an ancient phrase dating back to the Greek historian Plutarch writing in 100 CE: "He is a fool who lets slip a bird in the hand for a bird in the bush." Versions of it exist in German and most Romance languages. Cervantes's *Don Quixote* helped to spread the saying: "A little bird in the hand is worth more than a flying vulture" (*Mas vale pájaro en mano que buytre volando*). A Korean version of this goes, "Pursuing the running rabbit and lost the one already caught."

Give him an inch and he'll take a mile.

Once people said, "Give him an inch and he'll take an ell," but then they forgot what an ell was. It was a unit of measurement corresponding to "the forearm to the tip of the middle finger." As you can imagine, this method was none too precise. (Of course, most of our metric-system-using friends across the globe are as confused by how many inches are in a mile, as we are by ells.) The Italians make it a bit more corporeal: "Give a finger and they'll take a mile" (*A chi dai il dito si prende anche il braccio*). The most amusing international version of this proverb, however, is Arabic: "We let him in and he brought his donkey, too!"

Have your cake and eat it, too.

Something is wrong with this phrase, which means you can't have it both ways. You can, in fact, have cake and eat it. What you can't do is eat it and then still have it. That is how the saying used to go, but somehow we turned it around. Nigerian English retains the old form of the proverb "You can't eat your cake and have it." They're more logical in Nigeria.

~ *Around the World* ~

Being too greedy, you end up in a chicken trap.

(Taiwanese) Greed has consequences.

The greedy hawk eagle split its crotch.

(Japanese) Serious consequences.

This person looks after money as njuu look after locusts.

(Kikuyu: *Aikaragia mbia ta njũũ ngigĩ.*) A njuu is a bird that accompanies migrating locusts to feed on them.

- 162 -

49 ~ Poverty

Blood from a stone.

"You can't get blood from a stone" is an ancient phrase meaning you can't do the impossible. It was recorded in Italian writer Giovanni Torriano's *Second Alphabet*, 1662, as "to go about to fetch bloud out of stones." These days it is almost exclusively used in the context of trying to get money from someone who has none. The same expression is used in a number of Romance languages, including Italian and Spanish.

Robbing Peter to pay Paul.

People have been robbing Peter to pay Paul since the invention of debt. This saying, which means to take money for one thing and use it for another, has been in the language since the 1300s when English looked like this, "Lord, hou shulde God approve that thou robbe Petur, and gif this robbere to Poule in the name of Crist?" It is just as old in French and probably comes from the Latin where you find the phrase "As it were that one would crucify Paul in order to redeem Peter." Akan speakers in Ghana have their own version: "Someone has collapsed a wall to build another wall" (*W'ato ban agye ban*).

~ *Around the World* ~

A boxwood comb for a bald head.
(Turkish: *Kel başa şimşir tarak.*) An unnecessary luxury.

To put one's teeth on the shelf.
(Russian) Broke. You no longer need teeth if you have no food to eat.

What is got by begging is dear bought.
(Spanish: *No hay cosa tan cara como la que con ruegos se compra.*) This saying exists in most Romance languages.

Had the chicken had a hoe, it would have worked wonders on the dung heap.
(Yoruba) One's accomplishments are limited by one's means, rather than by one's ability.

~ 50 ~
Knowledge & Ignorance

Ignorance is bliss.

Most people who say this do not realize they are quoting the last line of an eighteenth-century poem. (That was back when people read and recited poems for fun.) The next time someone says this, you can increase your snob cred by mentioning the English poet Thomas Gray. "Ah," you can say, quoting the title, "Ode on a Distant Prospect of Eton College." Then you can say how much you appreciate the poem's evocative rendering of youthful nostalgia. Finish up by quoting the last stanza in full:

Since sorrow never comes too late,
And happiness too swiftly flies.
Thought would destroy their paradise.
No more; where ignorance is bliss,
'Tis folly to be wise.

Then ask your companion if she prefers Gray's works to those of his contemporary Alexander Pope. This will probably not win you any friends, but it will make you feel just a bit superior.

This ain't my first rodeo.

"I have experience in this area." A folksy version of "I wasn't born yesterday," the British phrase "I didn't come down with the last shower," and its more urban cousin "I was born at night, but not last night." The rodeo variant was a line of dialogue in the 1981 film *Mommie Dearest*. The Joan Crawford character says, "This ain't my first time at the rodeo." Unlike the widely parodied line "No wire hangers ever!" this one became an enduring part of the lexicon.

~ *Around the World* ~

Did you fall from a Christmas tree?

(Polish: *Z choinki się urwałaś?*) You are obviously uninformed.

He who does not recognize the falcon, grills it.

(Arabic) Ignorant people commit regrettable deeds. Falcons are for falconry. Chickens are for grilling.

We say, "It's a bull"; he says, "Milk it!"

(Arabic) Refers to the type of person who does not want to be confused with facts.

The dumbest farmer gets the biggest potato.

(German: *Die dümmsten Bauern ernten die dicksten Kartoffeln.*) Stupid people always win.

He has wind in his head.

(Russian) Said of someone who has a wooshing sound where his thoughts ought to be.

. . . .

WHAT DID YOU JUST SAY?

There is a Chinese proverb that says, "Give your tongue a roll and your knowledge will increase by one book." What does it mean?

A. Being well-fed is more important than being well-read.

B. Be willing to ask questions.

C. Teachers learn from their students.

D. Free sushi!

. . . .

ANSWER: B. If you are not afraid to ask questions, you will learn much faster.

~ 51 ~

Education

Experience is the best teacher.

The best way to learn is to do a thing yourself. People
have believed this since Roman times, because the saying
was borrowed from the Latin phrase "experience teaches"
(*experientia docet*). Scientists have tested this theory.
Researchers at the University of Washington found that infants
who were given a plastic cane to get an out-of-reach toy
understood the goal of a person using a similar tool better than
infants who had only watched an adult demonstrate it.

School of hard knocks.

Learning through adversity rather than formal schooling. The
first time this phrase appeared in print was in an 1871 directory
of ad men called "Men Who Advertise." The actual line was
"Trained, however, in the school of hard knocks, he now had
learned the theory of success." The advertisers may not have
coined the phrase, but if you want to spread a saying, you could

do worse than to put it in front of an audience of professional publicists. The Dutch phrase this same idea as "educated by damage and shame" (*door schade en schande wijs geworden*).

C'EST WHAT?!

BLACK ALPHABET EQUAL TO BUFFALO.

This is a far too literal translation of a Hindi proverb (*Kala akshar bhains barabar*) that makes it sound like a math exercise written by Salvador Dalí. (If black alphabet is equal to buffalo, how long does it take a centipede with a wooden leg to kick a hole through a ripe cucumber? Answer: No matter how dark the night, she's still your mother.) What it is actually saying is that if you can't read, letters are as meaningless to you as they would be to a buffalo.

A bunch of Philistines.

Uneducated, unsophisticated oafs. The historical Philistines apparently had a nice, well-organized town, and they were major traders in olive oil. So what gives? Is this a centuries-old ethnic slur? (See "Do You Know What You're Saying?" p. 248.) Their name translates into something like "of another tribe." This makes sense. Historically, nearly every tribe called themselves by a name that meant something like "the people."

When they came into contact with another tribe, they invariably dubbed those guys something like "the others," "the invaders," "the foreigners," or "those idiots over there." The Philistines are mentioned in the Bible as threatening invaders, but that is not the source of the idea that Philistines were backward. That notion sprung from a university in Germany. In the year 1693, a student and a non-student got into a fight and the student ended up dead. This obviously created some animosity towards the townies on the part of the young scholars. In this trying time, a minister delivered a funeral oration that included a Bible verse that mentioned the Philistines. The sermon must have been memorable because the students started to refer to it and eventually to use "Philistine" as an insider reference to non-students. (So "Philistine," meaning an uncultured boor, was not racist. It was classist.) In 1797 the German writers Johann Wolfgang Goethe and Friedrich Schiller used the term in a publication called *Vorsatz*, describing their critics as Philistines and defining it as "old-fashioned rationalists . . . who had no feeling for contemporary poetry." From there it made its way to England via writings about German authors. It started to gain currency in English in the 1860s. The English poet and critic Matthew Arnold probably popularized it.

Around the World

Experience keeps no school. She teaches her students singly.
(Russian) You don't really learn something until you have experienced it yourself.

A conversation with a wise person is worth ten years of study.
(Chinese) This is usually said as a compliment to someone with whom you have just had a conversation.

Not everyone who has ridden a horse is a horseman.
(Arabic) Just because you have done something does not mean you are an expert.

FALSE FRIENDS

In English, to say someone is a fathead is the same as saying he is an idiot. If he has a swollen head, he is arrogant. Not so in French. If you say someone is "a big head" (*une grosse tête*), it is a compliment. It means he is very smart.

~52~
Comprehension

In one ear and out the other.

Said of something that is spoken but makes no impression on the mind. The image evoked is obvious, and the saying dates back at least to the year 1400 when a version of it appeared in a poem. In Czech they say, "Like water on a duck's back" (*Jedním uchem tam, druhým ven*), a reference to the way water beads off a duck's feathers without penetrating.

It's all Greek to me.

Incomprehensible. This phrase goes all the way back to a medieval Latin proverb: "It is Greek; it cannot be read" (*Graecum est; non potest legi*). Therefore, you'll find versions of it in most Romance languages. The Spanish version is "speak in Greek" (*hablar en griego*). This may be the origin of the word "gringo" for those confusing outsiders. Meanwhile, in Czech they say, "It's a Spanish village to me" (*Je to pro mne španělská vesnice*).

HUH?

Have you ever had one of those moments where you stared at someone who was speaking and wondered if he was a genius or you were a nitwit? People experience this all over the world.

ICELANDIC

I come completely from the mountains. (Ég kem alveg af fjöllum.)
I have no idea what you're talking about.

FRENCH

I am swimming. (Je nage.)
"I'm totally lost." Roughly equivalent to the English "I am in over my head."

GERMAN

I only understand the train station. (Ich verstehe nur Bahnhof.)
Pretty much "I don't understand a word you are saying." That makes two of us.

～ Around the World ～

To blow little ducks.
(Latvian: *Pūst pīlītes.*) To spout nonsense or tell lies.

You speak French like a Spanish cow.
(French: *Parler français comme une vache espagnole.*) This is not a compliment. Spanish cows do not speak French all that well.

Columbus's egg.
(Italian: *Uovo di Colombo.*) An idea that is so simple and obvious that the person who needs it most can't see it.

WHAT DID YOU JUST SAY?
When a Dutch person says she is "standing with a mouth full of teeth" (*met de mond vol tanden staan*), is she:

    A. Dumbfounded.
    B. Smiling like an idiot.
    C. Scared.
    D. Going to the dentist.

ANSWER: A. She is standing slack-jawed.

~ 53 ~
Opinions

To each his own.

A shortened version of a phrase borrowed from the French "to each his own taste." In a similar vein, the French also say, "Tastes and colors are not discussed," often shortened to "tastes and colors" (*les goûts et les couleurs*). In Turkey they say, "Everyone has his own way of eating yogurt" (*Her yiğidin ayrı bir yogurt yiğişi vardır*). And if you criticize something your Hindi-speaking friend has done or made, she might respond with a sarcastic "What would a monkey know of the taste of ginger?"

Agree to disagree.

Someone is tired of arguing. "We'll have to agree to disagree" is what you say when two people who have irreconcilable opinions discover that neither is going to back down, and they would rather stop the discussion than challenge the other person to a duel. According to the 1948 book *Notes and Queries*, the phrase can be found in a 1770 sermon by English minister and theologian John Wesley, the founder of Methodism. He put the saying in quotes, which means he probably did not originate it.

THEY MAY HAVE A POINT

We have a lot of expressions urging us to stay true to our own point of view and not be swayed by the crowd. That is all well and good, but there are times when it behooves you to listen.

ROMANIAN

If two people say you're drunk, go to sleep. (Dacă doi spun că eşti beat, du-te şi te culcă.)
And if sixty people say you're drunk, it might be time for the twelve steps.

FRENCH

If everyone says you are an ass, bray! (Si tous disent que tu es un âne, brais!)
Versions of this saying appear in Italian, Spanish, Portuguese, and Romanian.

~ 54 ~
Opposites

Opposites attract.

If this axiom is to be believed, two people who have absolutely nothing in common are the most likely to develop romantic feelings for one another. *"Vive la différence!"* as the French say. We certainly accept this premise in our romantic comedies. If a man and a woman hate each other in the first scene, you can bet there will be a marriage proposal by the end. Interestingly, in Poland they say, "Same kinds attract" (*Swój ciągnie do swojego*). Haven't they seen *You've Got Mail*? It turns out the Poles are right. Study after study has shown that, in fact, people choose romantic partners who are similar to them in age, cultural background, political views, religion, and social class. Even if they are not that much alike, studies show that the more they believe they are alike, the better is the chance that the couple will last.

Comparing apples and oranges.

Sometimes shortened to "it's like apples and oranges." Two things that are so different no comparison is possible. Of course, any two things can be compared. "The sky has these things in common with a turnip and these differences . . ." If you ever wondered why two round fruits are used as uncomparable objects, you were not the first. In 1995 Scott Sandford, a NASA researcher, set out to prove that the two objects can be compared, and he published his results in *The Annals of Improbable Research*. After producing a spectrograph of dried samples of an apple and an orange, he concluded that it was quite easy to compare the two. "Thus, it would appear that the comparing apples and oranges defense should no longer be considered valid. This is a somewhat startling revelation," Sandford wrote. "It can be anticipated to have a dramatic effect on the strategies used in arguments and discussions in the future." The Turkish compare apples and pearls (*elmayla armutu mukayese etmek*). The Chinese meanwhile say, rather sensibly, "A bridge is a bridge and a road is a road." Like apples and oranges, you shouldn't confuse one with the other.

Like chalk and cheese.

Two things that are superficially alike but entirely different in their important qualities. The earliest example was from English poet John Gower's *Confessio Amantis* of 1393, which refers to a dishonest merchant adulterating his product: "And thus ful ofte chalk for cheese he changeth with ful littel cost." It is an odd expression, but not nearly as strange as its Taiwanese counterpart "comparing chicken droppings to tofu." Similar proverbs appear in many languages, but no two use the same two objects. The Japanese compare mud and clouds. The Chinese, beggars and gods.

WHAT DID YOU JUST SAY?

There is a Greek saying that begins "life is like a cucumber." In what way?

   A. It is full of seeds so that when it is destroyed it creates new life.

   B. You sometimes find worms inside.

   C. Some people like it, some people don't.

   D. You never know what you're going to get.

ANSWER: C. The full saying is "Life is like a cucumber, one person eats and is refreshed, another person eats and struggles." This is to say life is what you make it. (D is a catchphrase from the movie *Forrest Gump*.)

~ 55 ~

Art

Art is long, life is short.

The idea here is that works of art are far more enduring than a single human lifespan. This is true of the works of Shakespeare but perhaps less so of the works of Justin Bieber. When the proverb was first written by the Greek physician Hippocrates in the fourth century BCE, it had a slightly different meaning. It meant that life was too short to ever achieve full mastery. As the English poet Geoffrey Chaucer translated it in 1380, "The lyf so short, the craft so long to lerne." It is often quoted in its Latin form, "*Ars longa, vita brevis.*"

Art for art's sake.

Art that serves no useful purpose besides being art. First coined by the French philosopher Victor Cousin as "l'art pour l'art." The concept, if not the actual words, were popularized by Théophile Gautier, who reflected on Cousin's ideas in the preface to his novel *Mademoiselle de Maupin*. The notion that art should have no utilitarian purpose was highly influential among the leading lights of the British aesthetic movement, including writers Walter Pater, Oscar Wilde, and Samuel Taylor Coleridge. The English translation "art for art's sake" became their slogan. It was, and is, equally often used as criticism by those who don't appreciate the artistic merits of, say, a frame with an orange square in the middle.

The poor craftsman blames his tools.

This cliché is as old and widespread as it is true. The French have been saying, "A bad workman will never find a good tool" (*Mauves ouvriers ne trovera ja bon hostill*) since the thirteenth century. The Spanish novelist Miguel de Cervantes wrote, "Tis an ill workman that quarrels with his own tools" in his classic seventeenth-century masterpiece *Don Quixote*. Today, the Spanish are fond of saying, "The poor writer blames his pen" (*El mal escribano le echa la culpa a la pluma*). It's hard to know how long the Germans have been saying, somewhat sarcastically, "If the horseman is bad, it's the horse's fault" (*Wenn der Reiter nichts taugt, ist das Pferd schuld*), though you can bet it dates back to the beginning of the bumpy ride.

~ Around the World ~

Never confuse art with life.

(Japanese) The contestants on your favorite reality shows are not really your friends.

And now, an entry that doesn't fit any category:

NEITHER FISH NOR FOWL.

Neither one thing nor another. Something that doesn't fit in any category. This is how, we express it today, but in the olden days people tried to categorize their proteins by saying "neither flesh nor fish" or "neither fish, nor flesh, nor good red-herring," which is much more poetic, but a bit of a mouthful for everyday speech. I am partial to the Russian version of this saying, which is "neither two nor one and a half."

~ 56 ~
Music

Music has charms to soothe the savage breast.

Or music hath charms to soothe the savage *beast*. This is an oft-misquoted literary allusion. In fact, it is more often misquoted than correctly quoted. It was originally written by the English playwright William Congreve in *The Mourning Bride*, 1697.

Musick has Charms to sooth a savage Breast,
To soften Rocks, or bend a knotted Oak.
I've read, that things inanimate have mov'd,
And, as with living Souls, have been inform'd,
By Magick Numbers and persuasive Sound.

Play by ear.

This one sounds strange to foreigners. It does not mean using your ear to play, although violinists sometimes look as if they do. It just takes the ear as a stand-in for what it does: hear. So "playing by ear" means playing what you hear, without sheet music. The earliest incidence of the term "playing by ear" recorded in the *Oxford English Dictionary* was in a 1658 text by the British composer and author of music theory texts (the appropriately named) John Playford. In *An Introduction to the Skill of Musick* he wrote: "To learn to play by rote or ear without book."

Elevator music.

Much-maligned innocuous background music played in public places, such as elevators. The practice of piping music into elevators was more common in the past than it is today. It is most often used for comic effect these days in movies when, for example, a chase is interrupted by some calm music when the characters take an elevator. (A cinematic cliché.) Elevator music dates back to the 1930s when the company Muzak sold America on the idea that pleasant background music increased productivity. The phrase "elevator music" itself did not come into common use until the 1970s. The earliest example I found in a newspaper database search was from 1963. Earl Wilson quoted Victor Borge: "'Did you hear about the man who wouldn't live anywhere in the hotel except the first floor?' He smiled as he was making up the joke. 'Why?' I asked, playing the straight man. 'Because he couldn't stand the music they played in the elevator.'" "Elevator music," "airplane music," and "factory music" are all pretty monstrous. . . . The idea that music in elevators would increase productivity is particularly American, and so is this expression.

~ Around the World ~

You sing like an elephant farted in your ear.
(Croatian: *Pjevaš kao da ti je slon prdnuo u uho.*) It means you have no ear for music, obviously.

Did an elephant stomp on your ear?
(Polish: *Słoń nastąpił ci na ucho?*) It also means you have no ear for music.

To polish belt buckles.
(Central American Spanish: *Pulir hebillas.*) To dance closely.

FALSE FRIENDS

It might sound like the Italian expression "to do the string to someone" (*fare il filo a qualcuno*) should be equivalent to wooing someone with the music of a stringed instrument, or at least stringing someone along. Don't be fooled. Having the string on someone means to look at him in such a way as to draw him in with your eyes. In English "to have your eye on someone." Also, in Spanish "to have wood" (*tener madera*) means "to have what it takes," not what it means in English.

~ 57 ~
Communication &
Speech

Call a spade a spade.

To speak the truth plainly. To call a thing what it is, as opposed to, say, calling a spade a "combat emplacement evacuator," as a Department of Veterans Affairs document once referred to a shovel. It is a truly ancient saying going all the way back to Plutarch's *Apophthegmata* in 178 BCE. The French have the same idea, but say "to call a cat a cat" (*appeler un chat un chat*).

Another county (or nation) heard from.

A comment made when someone has been listening to a debate or argument and then finally joins the fray. They probably have no idea that they are making an allusion to the 1876 U.S. presidential election. Ten points if you can name the candidates. No? It was Rutherford B. Hayes against Samuel J. Tilden. The election was a nail-biter. Like the *Bush v. Gore* contest of recent memory, it was too close to call. There was a recount, and the process dragged out for several months, and the public grew weary of the process. Each time another result came in, someone would say, "Another county heard from." The saying stuck and even morphed into "Another nation heard from." (This is the version my grandmother used to say.)

WHAT DID YOU JUST SAY?

In Ibibio they use the phrase "narrate the story to a deaf man" (*buk mbuk wut inan*). What does it mean?

    A. To fall on deaf ears.
    B. To do something pointless.
    C. To be stubborn.
    D. I'm interested in what you are saying.

ANSWER: D. If you use this phrase, you are asking the person to repeat the story in greater detail. "Tell me more."

Your call is important to us.

Unless you just arrived from Mars, you have heard this as you waited on hold, along with "We are experiencing higher than average call volume" and "A representative will answer your call in the order in which it was received." Its use persists even though most people do not believe it and respond with "If my call were important to you, you'd have a human being answer it!" The expression itself probably predates hold music and messages. The first music-on-hold patent was filed in 1962. In 1964 we find the following notice in an Indiana newspaper: "McGill Manufacturing has an interesting and most helpful fold-over brochure. . . . Inside the fold, under the words 'your call is important to us,' is a wealth of information on the best times to call on executives. . . ." Note that "calling" here means an in-person visit. It did not become the ubiquitous and much-maligned phrase it is today, however, until the mid-1980s.

WHAT DID YOU JUST SAY?

Your Xhosa-speaking friend leans in and whispers in your ear, "Let us put our mouths together" (*Makhe sifakane imilomo*). What is she suggesting?

A. Let's discuss this privately.

B. Let's kiss.

C. Let's get married.

D. Let's eat.

ANSWER: A. She only wants to talk to you. Don't get the wrong idea.

~ *Around the World* ~

To jump from the rooster to the donkey.

(French: *Passer du coq à l'âne.*) This French idiom refers to an abrupt change in topic. You can use it to describe someone who is hard to follow because he wanders from subject to subject, or you can use it about yourself, for example: "I know I'm jumping from rooster to donkey here, but did you see the game last night?"

With overchurning, you will get poison.

(Bengali) Talking about an interesting subject for too long makes it dull. "I think we've beaten this topic to death."

To make something out of wood and paint it red.

(Estonian: *Puust ja punaseks ette tegema*.) To make something crystal clear.

To drive over someone's mouth.

(German: *Über den Mund fahren*.) To interrupt someone who is speaking.

To enter the enemy lines alone with only a sword.

(Japanese) To speak bluntly.

C'EST WHAT?!

TO HAVE A STICK IN YOUR EAR
(AT HAVE EN PIND I ØRET).

This Danish saying means you're not listening. To which the usual reply, one can only imagine, is "What? I can't hear you. I have a stick in my ear." This should on no account be confused with an American expression about a stick in another bodily orifice, which means to be uptight and rigid.

~ 58 ~

Silence & Brevity

Conspiracy of silence.

An agreement not to speak about something unpleasant or criminal. It was first coined in the nineteenth century among artists who grumbled about not finding an audience. The Welsh poet Lewis Morris once complained to Oscar Wilde that there was a conspiracy of silence that kept his works from being reviewed. When he asked Wilde what he should do, the Irish wit replied, "Join it."

In a nutshell.

In a concise way. The roots of the expression are deep. They go back to Pliny the Elder in 77 CE. Pliny wrote that the great philosopher Cicero had seen a copy of the *Iliad* written on a piece of parchment that was so small it could be fit into a walnut shell. Shakespeare's *Hamlet* uses the image when he says, "I could be bounded in a nutshell, and count myself a king of infinite space, were it not that I have bad dreams." Even so, it was not until the nineteenth century that "in a nutshell" became a popular way to refer to a compact thought.

Silence is golden.

Versions of this saying go back to ancient Egypt, but it came to English via a translation of a German text by Scottish writer Thomas Carlyle in his 1831 novel *Sartor Resartus*. "Speech, too, is great, but not the greatest. As the Swiss Inscription says: '*Sprecfien ist silbern; Schweigen ist golden*' (Speech is silvern; Silence is golden); or as I might rather express it: Speech is of Time, Silence is of Eternity." The joys of silence were a common theme for Carlyle, who also once wrote, "Under all speech that is good for anything, there lies a silence that is better. Silence is deep as Eternity; speech is shallow as Time." But what was this fabled "Swiss Inscription"? No one really knows, and it seems scholars and linguists have spent some time trying to figure it out. They have suggested similar Persian, Arabic, North African, Dutch, and German proverbs as Carlyle's source.

~ *Around the World* ~

Words are like a parcel: If you tie lots of knots, you will have to undo them.

(Malagasy: *Ny teny toy ny fonosana, ka izay mamono no mamaha.*) Choose your words carefully. They also say, "Oxen are trapped by their horns and men by their words" (*Ny omby singorana amin'ny tandrony, ary ny olona kosa amin'ny vavany*).

If the fool knew how to be silent, he could sit among the wise.
(Persian) See "Put your foot in your mouth," (p. 127).

Who says nothing consents.
(French: *Qui ne dit mot consent*.) Versions of this saying exist in many languages.

WILL YOU PLEASE BE QUIET?

"VERBOSITY LEADS TO UNCLEAR, INARTICULATE THINGS." —DAN QUAYLE.

You know that person who speaks whatever comes into his mind, blathers on ceaselessly about nothing at all, and just keeps on talking long after he should have finished a sentence, but he just can't seem to get to a full stop so you can get a word in edgewise, you know what I'm saying? Sure. We all do. There are expressions for these sorts all over the world. In Japan they say such a person is "born mouth first." The Basques say he is "a word bucket" (*hitzontzia da*). Cantonese speakers say, "Even when dead, the mouth will still be left."

~ 59 ~

Indecision

To hedge one's bets.

This is a reference to a bushy hedge that can serve as
protection. "Hedging a bet" is to make multiple bets or choices
in order to win no matter what the outcome: avoiding a single
course of action. The French version is "to spread out one's
wagers" (*étaler ses paris*). In Italian it is "to wager for and
against" (*scommettere pro e contro*).

To sit on the fence.

To be undecided. If you're sitting on the fence, you're not in one
land or another, but at least you're sitting on something. If you're
German, you have to hover in midair because their version
of this saying is "to sit between two chairs" (*zwischen swei
Stühlen sitzen*).

～ Around the World ～

Hold a chess piece and not know what move to make.

(Chinese) This is why they invented the chess-move timer.

To spare both the goat and the cabbage.

(French: *Ménager la chèvre et le chou.*) Instead of making cabbage soup and letting the goat live, or feeding the cabbage to the goat and eating it, the indecisive Frenchman spares both.

He just carries things around.

(Navajo) This character has a lot of tools but is wandering around not knowing what to do with them.

~ 60 ~
Exclamations

Great Scott!

This expression of surprise or amazement originated as a substitute for "Great God!" in an era (the 1800s) when taking the Lord's name in vain was considered a much more serious offense than it is today. Etymologists posit that the "Scott" was American general William Winfield Scott, who led the American troops in the Mexican War of 1846–1848. Today it is most associated with the character Doc Brown in the *Back to the Future* movies. (The expression is spoken in the trilogy sixteen times. Fans count things like that.)

Holy cow!

There are a number of English exclamations beginning with the word "holy." Along with the cow, we have "holy smoke" and "holy Moses." As with the above examples, this probably began as a tamer option to a blasphemy, although "holy Moses" is not entirely unblasphemous. The Spanish get in on this phrasing, too, as they are fond of exclaiming "holy God" (*Dios santo*) and "holy Heaven" (*cielo santo*).

~ *Around the World* ~

Oh, you fat father.
(German) A mild expression of surprise with similar force to "good heavens."

Monkeys bite me!
(Portuguese: *Macacos me mordam!*) An expression of surprise or amazement.

SACRE BLEU!

This is an antiquated curse in French, a milder substitute for the blasphemous *sacré Dieu*, or "sacred God." Whenever the English want to evoke the image of a surprised Frenchman, they use this phrase. The French, au contraire, do not use it and haven't since the nineteenth century or so. It is a bit like a modern-day Londoner saying, "Dash it all!" when he stubs his toe.

~ 61 ~

Humor

You're pulling my leg.

"You're joking!" The best theory as to why we say this is that back in the bad old days thieves would trip their intended victims with a hook, literally pulling on someone's leg to make them fall. From there, the idea of trying to trip someone up morphed into this weird cliché. Russians do not pull legs. They say, "I'm not hanging noodles on your ears" for the same effect.

Tongue-in-cheek.

A humorously ironic statement. Word-watchers posit that this was once a bit of stagecraft and that an actor would literally stick his tongue against the inside of his cheek to indicate he was joking. The Germans have long understood the power of humor, saying, "Many true words are spoken in jest" (*Im scherz klopft man oft, und im Ernst wird auf*) since at least the fourteenth century.

~ Around the World ~

Jaw dislocated.

(Japanese) To laugh like crazy.

WHAT DID YOU JUST SAY?

Your French friend says she had banged her butt on the ground (*se taper le cul par terre*). What does she mean?

    A. She is clumsy.

    B. She was laughing like crazy.

    C. She is frustrated.

    D. She wants to know if those slacks make her look fat.

ANSWER: B. She was laughing like crazy. A bit like ROFLMAO.

~ 62 ~

Success

Pull a rabbit out of a hat.

To achieve something seemingly impossible, as if by magic. It's a
reference to the most iconic of magic tricks—pulling a live rabbit
out of a top hat. The first magician to pull a rabbit out of a hat
was Harry Blackstone Sr. He would produce a live rabbit from a
hat and then put it in a box and give it to a child in the audience.
When the child opened the box later, she would find that the
rabbit had been transformed into a bag of candy. A more intense
Japanese version of this is "wake from death and return to life."

To run circles around someone.

To be much better than the other person. The image here is
of a footrace in which one runner is so slow that his opponent
could run forward, circle back and run forward again, and still
come out victorious. The saying dates back to England in the
mid-1800s, where it began as a reference to hunting hounds
that would run rings around their prey. A similar idiom is to be

"head and shoulders above" someone. It came into being around the same time, but as it was originally used, it referred only to the literally tall. His head and shoulders would tower above a shorter person.

C'EST WHAT?!

PUTTING MISO ON THE ASS OF DAIKOKU.

This is a Japanese phrase, but whatever could it mean? Does it help to know that miso is soybean paste and that Daikoku is the god of wealth? I didn't think so.

It means adding to something that is already nearly perfect. "Gilding the lily" or "putting a cherry on top." An Icelandic way of saying that something good just got better is "There's a raisin at the end of the sausage"(*Það er rúsínan í pylsuendanum*).

A win-win situation.

A situation that benefits parties on both sides of a dispute or negotiation. The earliest reference I was able to find to a "win-win situation" in a newspaper database search was in 1949. (There were occasional references before that to a "win, win spirit," in which win was used twice for emphasis.) The phrase didn't rise to the level of cliché until the late 1960s when it was a catchphrase in "sensitivity labs." "Instead of a win-lose situation, we want a win-win situation," explained the facilitator of such a group in a 1970 article, suggesting that not everyone was familiar with the idea yet. Use of the phrase seems to have reached its apex in about 1997, although it is still overused to this day.

WHAT DID YOU JUST SAY?

Your Hungarian friend tells you "the fence is not made of sausage" (*nem kolbászból van a kerítés*). What is she saying?

    A. Prepare for disappointment.

    B. The neighbors will gossip.

    C. She is not rich.

    D. You can't bluff your way through this.

ANSWER: A. It means something is not as great as it seems because, come on, what could be as good as a fence made out of sausage?

~ 63 ~
Dreams &
Ambitions

To build castles in the air.

To have unrealistic ambitions; to dream of a fantastical future. Before we were building proverbial castles in the stratosphere, we were building them in Spain. Back in the 1400s there must have been something quite romantic in the notion of the Iberian peninsula, because both the French and the English used this expression. In English it was "to make castellis in Spaygne," and in French "*bâtir des chateaux en Espagne.*" By the mid-1500s, Spain lost its luster and the castles migrated upwards. They say the same thing in Germany, or nearly so: "To build air castles" (*Luftschlösser bauen*).

Too big for his britches (breeches).

An arrogant person. The phrase was first used in print in *An Account of Col. Crockett's Tour to the North and Down East*, 1835, written by Davy Crockett. "I myself was one of the first to fire a gun under Andrew Jackson. I helped to give him all his glory. But I liked him well once: but when a man gets too big for his breeches, I say Good bye." The idea of making an arrogant person comical by picturing him swelling out of tiny clothes is international.

~ Around the World ~

She has a bird to urge her along.
(Xhosa: *Unentaka yokuzigqatsa.*) She is ambitious.

If I am cooking meat in my dream, why would I not add ghee generously?
(Bengali) Ghee is expensive, so this means that if you're fantasizing, why limit yourself?

To try to catch the moon's reflection in the middle of the water.
(Chinese) Unrealistic dreams. Similar in meaning to the English "build castles in the air."

Will the money seen in a dream meet one's expenses?
(Tamil) Sigh. I guess you're going to have to get out of bed and go to work after all.

~ 64 ~
Intentions

The road to hell is paved with good intentions.
Used when something done for the right reasons turns out wrong or when someone had his heart in the right place but failed to act. The nineteenth-century Anglican archbishop and poet Richard Chenevix Trench called this "perhaps the queen of all proverbs." This saying is often attributed to St. Bernard. "Hell is full of good intentions or desires" (*L'enfer est plein de bonnes volontés ou désirs*). But the phrase is found nowhere in his writings. Earlier versions omitted "the road," and so Hell itself was full of good intentions. The paved versions may have been influenced by the biblical verse: "The way of sinners is made plain with stones, but at the end thereof is the pit of hell." You find versions of this proverb in several European languages.

The best laid plans of mice and men.
The unsaid part of this cliché is "often go wrong." This comes from the poem "To a Mouse" by eighteenth-century Scottish

writer Robert Bruns who turned over a nest of field mice with his plow and wondered at how fate interfered with the plans of men as it had with those mice.

> *But Mousie, thou are no thy-lane,*
> *In proving foresight may be vain:*
> *The best laid schemes o' Mice an' Men,*
> *Gang aft agley,*
> *An' lea'e us nought but grief an' pain,*
> *For promis'd joy!*
> *Still, thou art blest, compar'd wi' me!*
> *The present only toucheth thee:*
> *But Och! I backward cast my e'e,*
> *On prospects drear!*
> *An' forward, tho' I canna see,*
> *I guess an' fear!*

~ Around the World ~

Talk about next year and the devil will laugh.
(Japanese) The world will not bend to your intentions.

The day he arranged the corn in the granary, he did not think in terms of the rat.
(Yoruba) This could be said of a poor planner but also contains a warning that you can't foresee everything.

Putting a gold leaf on the back of the Buddha image.
(Thai) Doing a good deed without seeking attention or praise.

~ 65 ~
Ability

To be all thumbs.

Clumsy. Now a cliché, it is a vivid image when you stop to really picture it. The English writer John Heywood wrote in his 1546 collection of proverbs, "When he should get aught each finger is a thumb." Navajo speakers have a similar evocative simile: "His hands are round like a ball" (*t'óó bila' dijool*). Both the Greek and the Germans attribute clumsiness to the left-handed. In German it is "to have two left hands" (*zwei linke Hände haben*)—an expression we occasionally use in English as well. In modern Greek it is simply to be left-handed. The Portuguese might be the most picturesque of all. They say, "To have spider hands" (*Ter mâos de aranha*).

In his wheelhouse.

In the past few years, "in his wheelhouse" has become the go-to phrase to mean a business's or individual's particular area of skill and talent. It seems to have arisen as "core competency" has waned. Literally, a wheelhouse is the pilothouse on a boat. That sense of the term has been around, according to the *Oxford English Dictionary*, since 1835. In the late 1950s, the wheelhouse became baseball jargon referring to the strike zone—a ball that is in just the right place for a batter to hit. This is the most likely path to the business world.

Around the World

We're four cats.

(Italian: *Siamo quattro gatti.*) In English this might mean "We are four cool dudes with a soft spot for the beat poets." In Italian it means "There are not enough of us to complete the task."

WHAT DID YOU JUST SAY?

"If your butt cannot take it, don't use that kind of laxative." This is a Taiwanese expression, but what does it mean?

    A. Your eyes are bigger than your stomach.

    B. If you can't stand that heat, stay out of the kitchen.

    C. Don't be greedy.

    D. Make a decision already!

ANSWER: B. It means not to take on a task that is beyond your ability. Another way of saying this is "Don't bite off more than you can chew." A Chinese way of saying this is "If you don't have the diamond tool, don't touch the porcelain work." In Malagasy it is "If you are just a dung beetle, don't try to move mountains" (*Aza manao herim-boantay*). And in Xhosa it is "Stop covering the bone when you are toothless" (*Yeka ukuthanda ihleza ungenamazinyo*).

~ 66 ~

Ease

More than one way to skin a cat.

I am not sure you need even one, but for hundreds of years people have been using metaphors of pet-killing to say there is more than one way to do a thing. A British version from the mid-1800s was "There are more ways of killing a cat than choking him with cream." Another version says, "There are more ways of killing a dog than choking him with pudding." The oldest known version comes from a collection of proverbs dated 1678: "There are more ways to kill a dog than hanging." This suggests that if you want to murder a house pet, the English are the people to call.

Piece of cake.

Why should "piece of cake" mean that something is easy? I can think of a lot of foods that are easier to make than cake. We should say "microwave popcorn." The Polish have the right idea when they say, "It's a roll with butter" (*Bułka z masłem*).

The Swedish think it is "easy as a pancake" (*lätt som en plätt*). Blame Ogden Nash, who wrote this line in his 1936 *Primrose Path*: "Her picture's in the papers now, and life's a piece of cake." In this context, the piece of cake is easy to eat, not make. It calls to mind the famous line attributed to Marie Antoinette, "Let them eat cake." In Nigerian English, "piece of cake" has a different meaning. It means your share of something. "He told the boss he was not getting his piece of cake."

Low-hanging fruit.

The metaphorical use of this phrase for that which can be obtained with the least amount of effort emerged in the business world in the late 1980s. But it is not just would-be executives who look for a big reward with a small effort. Tamil speakers have the saying, "Pull a mountain by tying a hair to it. If you succeed, you will get a mountain; if you lose, you will lose a hair." It means, you might as well give it a shot if it requires little effort. Ironically, the lowest hanging fruit is probably the strawberry. Farmers call it "the devil's fruit" because harvesting it is back-breaking labor due to the constant bending.

~ *Around the World* ~

The cat is unhappy that the rice is too hot.

(Bengali) When things come too easily for you, the slightest obstacle makes you unhappy.

WHAT DID YOU JUST SAY?

If a Dutch speaker says, "It is as if an angel is pissing on your tongue" (*Alsof er een engeltje over je tong piest*), what does he mean?

A. The meal is delicious.

B. You speak beautifully.

C. You are a great singer.

D. You are lucky.

ANSWER: A. Apparently angel piss tastes like champagne.

~ 67 ~

Luck

Break a leg.

Theater types have a lot of superstitions. It is bad luck to whistle or to say the name "Macbeth" instead of the euphemism "the Scottish play." Some actors hold that it is bad luck to say the last line of a play during dress rehearsal. It is also bad luck to wish an actor good luck. Instead they say, "Break a leg." The expression used in this sense is not as old as you might suppose. It was coined in the United States in the mid-twentieth century. The rather odd expression probably comes from the German. They say, "Break your neck and leg" (*Hals und Beinbruch*). Why would anyone say that? It seems to be a pun on the Hebrew blessing "*hatzlakha u-brakha,*" or "success and blessing." The theory is that the American variant, therefore, was imported by Jewish actors. There was, incidentally, an earlier use of the phrase "break a leg" back in the 1600s. It had nothing to do with luck and meant "to give birth to an illegitimate child." That sense is thankfully lost.

Cats have nine lives. / A cat always lands on its feet.

Cats look extremely lucky. They are able to survive falls that would kill any human, and they, indeed, usually land on their feet. They have flexible backbones with smaller vertebrae that allow them to twist in response to their righting reflex. They learn to master the trick when they are only seven weeks old. There are actually recorded cases of cats falling from skyscrapers in earthquakes and surviving. But hey, we've got the opposable thumbs, so it's a trade-off.* In Italy they say a lucky person has "seven lives like a dog."

Luck of the Irish.

There is some debate as to whether the "luck of the Irish" is good luck or bad luck. In either case, it comes up a lot around St. Patrick's Day. What is most interesting is that it is not Irish at all. It is an Americanism. Edward T. O'Donnell, author of *1001 Things Everyone Should Know About Irish American History*, wrote: "During the gold and silver rush years in the second half of the nineteenth century, a number of the most famous and successful miners were of Irish and Irish American birth. . . . Over time this association of the Irish with mining fortunes led to the expression 'luck of the Irish.' Of course, it carried with it a certain tone of derision, as if to say, only by sheer luck, as opposed to brains, could these fools succeed."

---

* For more on the science of falling cats see: http://www.jareddiamond.org/Jared_Diamond/Further_Reading_files/Diamond%201989.pdf

~ Around the World ~

Into the mouth of the wolf.

(Italian: *In bocca al lupo*.) Good luck. It's really no stranger than saying "break a leg," when you think about it.

Good luck is like air—even if you close your door, it can get in and out freely.

(Luganda: *Omukisa mpewo—nobwoggalawo guyingira era gufuluma*.) A more optimistic view than our own "opportunity knocks once." In Uganda good luck will find you whether you let it in or not.

~ 68 ~
Swift Action

Strike while the iron is hot.

Act now! A blacksmith's metaphor. In order to work metal, you must heat it up until it is soft, then strike it on an anvil. If you wait too long, it cools down and can't be molded. This metaphor has occurred to people throughout the world. The same saying exists in most Romance languages, and the Chinese say almost exactly the same. Koreans say, "Pull out the bull's horn in a flash," because that is one thing you would not want to do slowly.

FALSE FRIENDS

There is a Chinese expression "Mend the leaking pot while it is already hot." Although this sounds a lot like the English "Strike while the iron is hot," it has a different meaning. To mend a broken pot while it is hot is to make the best of a bad situation.

Like a bat out of hell.

If you're in hell, you want to get out fast. Although why bats would be in any greater hurry to escape the place of weeping and gnashing of teeth than any other creature is a mystery. It is the imagery of how bats scatter when they are frightened that made this expression of fast flight stick. It most likely has a military origin. It first appears in print in the World War I novel *Three Soldiers* by the American author John Dos Passos. "We went like a bat out of hell along a good state road." (Teenagers started to sing it in the 1970s when Meatloaf used it in his hit song "Paradise by the Dashboard Light.") This is how you run when an enemy soldier is chasing you or if you've been caught doing something you should not. A Russian equivalent is "to run like a scorched cat."

WHAT DID YOU JUST SAY?

A Russian friend says, "If you called yourself a milk-mushroom, get into the basket." What on earth is she trying to tell you?

A. You're being arrogant.

B. Follow through on what you promise.

C. If you can't stand the heat, get out of the kitchen.

D. Soup is yummy.

ANSWER: B. Russians love mushroom hunting. If you say you're a mushroom, act like a mushroom, darn it.

~ *Around the World* ~

The day is worked while it is still fresh.
(Zulu: *Libunjwa liseva.*) This is sometimes translated with the English proverb, "Make hay while the sun shines."

Explode all the landmines.
(German: *Alle Minen sprengen lassen.*) To put in a great effort. To go all out.

~ 69 ~
Limits

The sky's the limit.

Unlimited opportunity. This phrase is often attributed to early English translations of Miguel de Cervantes's *Don Quixote*. "Observing the roof of the place where they were in to be somewhat too low for their purpose, they carried him into the backyard, which had no limits but the sky." It seems unlikely that this was the origin, however, for two reasons. The first is that the reference to the sky was not made in the same way. It was said in passing to refer to an unobstructed view. The second, and more important, reason is that if this was the origin, it took a really long time to catch on. Word-watchers didn't see evidence of its widespread use until the early twentieth century.

Push the envelope.

This has nothing to do with the things that you use to mail letters. It's an aeronautics term that was popularized in Tom Wolfe's 1979 book *The Right Stuff*. The envelope, in this context, is the outer boundary of the known limits for the safe performance of a plane under various conditions. Test pilots have to push those boundaries as part of their work. In the 1950s and 60s, this was called "pushing the edge of the envelope," but this was too much to say and it was condensed. It didn't move beyond the realm of technical jargon until Wolfe's book and the film based upon it became hits in the 1980s. Now it's a term used around the world.

Glass ceiling.

A level above which women find it hard to rise in a corporate setting. They can see what goes on above but cannot rise above, not through overt discrimination, but through various aspects of the corporate culture. This one can be credited to Gay Bryant, then editor of *Women's World* magazine, who first used the phrase in an interview with *Adweek*.

WHAT DID YOU JUST SAY?

A Spanish speaker says he has "thrown the house out the window" (*tirar la casa por la ventana*). What does that mean?

A. Spared no expense.

B. Turned himself into knots with worry.

C. Gone beyond what he thought he was capable of doing.

D. Made a fresh start.

ANSWER: A. He is saying money is no object.

~ 70 ~
Futility

Carrying coals to Newcastle.

Newcastle is in the heart of England's coal country. So to carry coals there would be an entirely wasted effort. It was a familiar English expression as far back as the sixteenth century when it appeared in a list of common sayings. Different countries have their own versions of this proverb. In Hungarian it is "taking water to the Danube" (*vizet hord a Danába*). In Portuguese it is "to sell honey to a beemaster" (*vender mel ao colmeeiro*). In Spanish it is "like taking oranges to Valencia" (*excomo llevar naranjas a Valencia*), and in Russian it is "going to Tula, taking his own samovar." Tula is famous as a center for manufacturing samovars, those large, metal Russian tea-making contraptions.

Wild-goose chase.

An aimless search for something unobtainable. It once was a real game, a Shakespearean-era version of Follow the Leader. It began with a horse race, and the winner became the leader.

The losers had to follow him wherever he went. This reminded observers of wild geese in flight, hence the name. You can find a reference to the game in *Romeo and Juliet*, when Mercutio says, "Nay, if thy wits run the wild-goose chase, I have done; for thou hast more of the wild-goose in one of thy wits than, I am sure, I have in my whole five: was I with you there for the goose?" People lost interest in playing wild-goose chase, but the name had lodged as a vain pursuit of something not even worth having.

Searching for a needle in a haystack.

A needle buried under a mound of hay would be nearly impossible to find, but it could be worse. At least you can breathe while you look. In many Asian languages (including Taiwanese, Japanese, Chinese, and Korean) you have to find that needle at the bottom of the sea. In English we've been searching for lost needles for hundreds of years, but we have not always been pawing through proverbial haystacks to find them. The *Oxford English Dictionary* records a number of early needle-hiding places including "to go looke a nedle in a medow" (1530), "gropeth in the dark to find a needle in a bottle of hay" (1592), and "Seeking we may say, A Needle in a Truss of Hay" (1711).

Around the World

A keg without a bottom.

(German: *Ein Fass ohne Boden.*) A lost cause.

More difficult than teaching a camel to jump.

(Turkish: *Deveye hendek atlatmaktan daha zor.*) Said of something that is basically impossible.

> ### WHAT DID YOU JUST SAY?
> "To salt the porcupine's intestine when it is already salty" is an expression from Ibibio. What would be the best English equivalent?
> **A.** Carrying coals to Newcastle.
> **B.** A spanner in the works.
> **C.** A stitch in time saves nine.
> **D.** To err is human.

ANSWER: A. It means to do something unnecessary. Wasted effort. Another international phrase on the theme is "He gives earrings to the one without ears."

~ 11 ~

Never

Not for all the tea in China.

Something you would not do, no matter how well you were compensated. How much is all the tea in China? About 855,190 metric tons a year. At commodity prices of $1.86 per kilogram, that is worth about $1,590,653,400. Impressive, but it pales in comparison to all the coffee in Brazil, which is worth about $6,645,461,089.

Once in a blue moon.

Rarely. The common explanation for the origin is that it refers to an astronomical phenomenon. When a full moon occurs twice in a calendar month, it is called a "blue moon." A "blue moon" in this sense was once even more rare. It originally meant the third full moon in a season that contains four full moons. A blue moon, calculated by this method, could happen only in the months of February, May, August, and November. So something that occurs only when the moon is blue is rare, indeed, and thus the expression was born. There is only one problem with this story. The expression predates the astronomical sense by more than a century. Originally the phrase meant that something happened when the moon was literally blue, essentially never. "Once in a blue moon" may have inspired the lunar expression, which is an Americanism first recorded in the 1930s, rather than the other way around. There are colorful ways to refer to rare events throughout the world. My personal favorite is the Italian "at every death of a pope" (*ogni morte di papa*).

When pigs fly.

It will never happen. The French express the same sentiment by saying, "When hens have teeth." "When hell freezes over" means the same, but it has a little more force to it. If someone says, "I am going to be elected president," and you say, "When pigs fly," you're expressing extreme doubt. If you respond, "When hell freezes over," you're implying you'll work to prevent it.

WHAT DID YOU JUST SAY?

If a French person tells you she will help you hang wallpaper on Saint-Glinglin's Day (*à la Saint-Glinglin*), when will she do it?

    A. Right away

    B. When she has free time

    C. A week from today

    D. Never

ANSWER: D. Saint Glinglin is a nonexistent saint. You're going to have to hang that wallpaper yourself.

Around the World

The mouse doesn't bite the thread here.

(German: *Da beißt die Maus keinen Faden ab.*) Nothing can be done. The image seems to be of a mouse stuck in a trap made of thread and not gnawing its way out.

AIN'T GONNA HAPPEN

These wordly expressions all mean that you're never gonna get it. Never, never, never.

FRENCH

When hens have teeth. (Quand les poules auront des dents.)
Jamais! (English has a similar expression with a different meaning—"rarer than hen's teeth.")

RUSSIAN

When a lobster whistles on top of a mountain.
Nikogda!

DUTCH

When the cows are dancing on the ice. (Als de koeien op het ijs dansen.)
Nooit!

~ 72 ~
Competence

Practice makes perfect.

In 2014 a British survey of two thousand people asked them to recall a piece of wisdom given to them by their parents when they were children. "Practice makes perfect" came in at the top of the list of influential nuggets of wisdom. (Followed by "Treat others how you'd like to be treated" and "If at first you don't succeed, try, try again.") Parents have been telling their children this since Roman times. The Latin version is "Use makes perfect" (*Uses promptos facit*). Most Romance languages have one of two variants of the Latin: "practice makes perfect" or "practice makes mastery" or "a master." It was adopted into English in the 1500s as "Use makes mastery." It became "perfect" in 1560 or so.

Can't cut the mustard.

Unable to handle a job. Etymologists are a bit stumped as to why we say this. They know that "mustard" was once slang for "the genuine article." So perhaps someone who can't cut the mustard is someone who is not up to the task of working on the central issue at hand. Such a person might be given a lesser condiment that they can't do much damage with. Mayonnaise perhaps. Maybe a person who could "cut the mustard" was "the mustard" or the real deal. "Can't hack it" is a variant on "cut the mustard."

It is the good swimmer who is most often drowned.

(Persian) A warning against complacency.

An apprentice near a temple will recite the scriptures untaught.

(Japanese) You are the product of your environment.

WHAT DID YOU JUST SAY?

Your Navajo friend tells you that a coworker "acts like coyote excrement." What does he mean?

    A. He is nasty.

    B. He is inexperienced.

    C. He lies around and does nothing.

    D. He is clingy.

ANSWER: B. It means that he is a puppy so inexperienced he doesn't yet know how to clean the excrement off his fur. An English equivalent would be "wet behind the ears." The Russians say, "The nose has not grown out," while the Japanese say, "Smelling of milk."

~ 73 ~
Fame

Fifteen minutes of fame.

Ephemeral celebrity. It comes from a quote attributed to the pop artist Andy Warhol: "In the future, everyone will be famous for fifteen minutes." He was first credited with the phrase in a brochure for an 1968 exhibition of his work in Sweden. There is some debate as to whether Warhol actually ever said it, but there is no question that a lot of us have said it since. The French give you a little more time, though, saying, "Everybody has their hour of glory" (*Tout le monde a leur heure de gloire*).

Flash in the pan.

Ephemeral celebrity that has waned. It's a reference to old flintlock muskets, which had a depression called a "pan" to hold the priming powder. When the gun was fired, a steel hammer struck a flint and ignited the powder, causing sparks and musket ballet to fly. They didn't always work, though. Sometimes the powder would flare up and flash in the pan, a brilliant but short-lived and ineffective show. This was also referred to as "hanging fire," which is sometimes used for failure, although not as often as it once was. A Swahili expression for something that starts with a bang and ends with a whimper is "A race on the floor ends at the edge" (*Mbio za sakafuni huishia ukingoni*).

To go viral.

To spread quickly through a social network, as a virus is spread. The word "virus" has been with us even before scientists identified the microscopic agent that we call a virus today. Originally it referred to pus. From there it was applied to anything that was infectious and nasty. Only in the twentieth century did it get its current meaning. In the 1970s, "virus" was metaphorically extended to include malicious computer code. The expression "go viral" used in the medical sense was not current until the 1980s. Marketers picked it up shortly thereafter and used it for the rapid spread of information by word of mouth. These days information is more rapidly spread through computer networks, but the idea remains the same. When a German wants to say that someone has done something so spectacular it has gained widespread attention, he says he has "invented gunpowder" (*das Pulver erfinden*). Mandarin has the expression "to shock people with one shout," and the Portuguese say, "To put a lance into Africa" (*Meter uma lança em Africa*). I am told this means roughly the same thing.

~ Around the World ~

He is asking for eyes.
(Xhosa: *Ucel' amehlo.*) He is showing off.

To suck the camera.
(Spanish: *Chupar camara.*) To seek media attention.

He likes to be looked at like a long-hairy goat.
(Zulu: *Uthanda ukubukwa njengesiyephu.*) Why Zulu speakers gaze with rapt attention at long-haired goats is a mystery, but this means he wants lots of attention.

~ 74 ~

Status

Blue blood.

For five centuries, the Moors ruled over Spain. Around the
time that the Spanish aristocrats of Castile began to reassert
themselves, they tried to distinguish themselves from the
darker-skinned Moors by calling themselves "*sangre azul*," or
"blue blood." It meant that their skin was pale enough to see
the blue veins beneath it. Eventually the phrase was applied to
nobles of other nations.

Noblesse oblige.

Yes, this is French, but it was adopted wholesale when French
was the lingua franca of the aristocracy. The translation would
be "nobility obliges," if anyone used it. It refers to a social
contract that the blue bloods had with the commoners. Being
well-born came with it the responsibility to help others who
were worse off.

Wrong side of the tracks.

A poor area. If someone is "born on the wrong side of the tracks," he comes from a disadvantaged background. It's an American expression dating back to the nineteenth century when a boom in railroads meant that towns were sometimes split in two, with a wealthier section on one side of the boundary and the poorer area on another. Today you might say, "On the wrong side of the fence of the gated community."

~ *Around the World* ~

To be born in good diapers.

(Spanish: *Criarse en buenos pañales*.) To be born with a silver spoon in your mouth.

~ 75 ~

Appearances

His bark is worse than his bite.

He will not follow up his (harsh) words with action. Many
languages use a variant of the saying "barking dogs seldom
bite." (It can be found in Taiwanese, Japanese, and Chinese.)
This version means not only that a particular person isn't as
imposing as he seems but also that you should worry more
about the one who is not putting on a show.

Keeping up with the Joneses.

The title of a comic strip that ran for twenty-six years in the
New York Globe in the 1900s. It came to mean trying to maintain
the same lifestyle and social status as one's neighbors, usually
by buying lots of expensive stuff. To which English writer Quentin
Crisp responded, "Never keep up with the Joneses. Drag them
down to your level; it's cheaper."

∽ Around the World ∽

Do not despise a man of small stature—he may be as strong as the kahikatoa.

(Maori: *He iti he iti kahikatoa.*) The kahikatoa is a small but strong tree.

He who conceals his disease cannot expect to be cured.

(Amharic) Twelve-step programs like AA have a similar catchphrase: "You're only as sick as your secrets."

He has a moon face.

(German: *Er hat ein Mondgesicht.*) This is used to describe someone ugly.

WHAT DID YOU JUST SAY?

"A sparrow that cries a lot has less than four ounces of meat." What is the best English equivalent to this Chinese phrase?

A. You can't judge a book by its cover.

B. Thinking outside the box.

C. A pig in a poke.

D. All bark and no bite.

ANSWER: D. The loudest bird is not the best to eat, just as the dog who barks loudest is not the fiercest. In Taiwan they say, "The frog blown up with air looks big but has little meat." The Korean version is "An empty cart makes more noise." The image is of an empty cart clattering over a rocky road. When it is weighted down with goods, it rattles less.

~ 76 ~
Beauty

Beauty is only skin deep.

A very old way to proclaim that beauty is a superficial value.
It dates back to a 1613 poem by the English poet Thomas
Overbury: "All the carnal beauty of my wife / Is but skin-deep." In
response, the author Jean Kerr famously quipped, "I'm tired of
all this nonsense about beauty being only skin-deep. That's deep
enough. What do you want, an adorable pancreas?"

Vanity (or beauty) knows no pain.

This is an expression that mothers use when they are pulling
snarls out of their daughters' hair. The Chinese version is "to look
beautiful, dressed scantily and freezing and screaming." One can
only assume that this nightmare scenario sounds more poetic in
Chinese than in its English translation.

CONTEXT MATTERS

In Taiwan there is a proverb that says, "Three parts substance, seven parts makeup." It means that it is important not to neglect the outer appearance—something along the lines of the English phrase "the clothes make the man."

But there is a time and a place for every wise saying. Albert F. Chang in *A Collection of Equivalent Proverbs in Five Languages* gave an example of someone getting it wrong. "During my college years," he wrote, "a classmate of mine one day on a date with his girlfriend . . . quoted the proverb saying: 'Oh, it is really true that three parts substance, seven parts makeup.' It is a natural consequence that the girl broke up with him. . . .'"

~ *Around the World* ~

Fish-fleshed.

(Turkish: *Balik etli*.) In Turkey this cliché compliments a woman's curves. If you were to say this to an American woman, she just might slap you.

WHAT DID YOU JUST SAY?

A French Canadian says, "You have water in the cellar" (*Avoir de l'eau dans la cave*). What does she mean?

A. You have a big bottom.

B. You are foolish.

C. Your pants are too short.

D. You have terrible taste in men.

ANSWER: C. You have outgrown your slacks, and they are too short. You may hear such clothing referred to in English as "floods" or "high-waters." The idea is that your pant leg is so high up your leg that it will not get wet in a flood.

~ 11 ~

Age

You can't teach an old dog new tricks.

As if to prove its own point, this is one of the oldest proverbs we've got. It's been doing its work in our language since at least 1534. It means that as people (or dogs) age they get stuck in their ways. Speakers of Romanian, however, believe you should listen to what the old dog says. "If the old dog barks," they say, "he gives counsel" (*Ciinele batrun nu latra la Luna*), meaning listen to your elders for good advice.

Youth is wasted on the young.

One of the great frustrations of life is that it takes so long to figure it all out, by the time you know what to do, your body is not up to the task. This phrase is often attributed to the Irish playwright George Bernard Shaw in the form "Youth is a wonderful thing. What a crime to waste it on children." The thing is, there is no evidence he actually wrote this. The quote was first attributed to him in a book of quotations in 1952. Dr.

Stanley Weintraub, who wrote a number of books on Shaw, suspects that this saying really belonged to Oscar Wilde. In any case, it is a useful truism. A French phrase on a similar theme is "If youth but knew, if old age but could" (*Si jeunesse savait, si vieillesse pouvait*).

～ Around the World ～

Demon of midday.

(French: *Le démon de midi.*) This is a poetic-sounding French way to refer to a midlife crisis. It is a biblical allusion referring to Psalm 91. In the English King James version it is worded, "Nor for the pestilence that walketh in darkness; nor for the destruction that wasteth at noonday."

Ocean thousand, mountain thousand.

(Japanese) Said of a person who has seen everything, but unlike the English "been there, done that," it has no world-weariness or boredom about it. This guy is mature, experienced, and super cool because he has seen and done it all, and all that knowledge has made him clever.

~ 78 ~

Death

Bite the dust.

This phrase, meaning "to die," sounds modern, but in fact it dates back to Homer, who used it in the *Illiad*: "May his fellow warriors . . . Fall round him to the earth and bite the dust." These days people are more familiar with the Queen song.

To die of a broken heart.

In everyday speech, when we say someone has a broken heart, we do not mean he is suffering from a myocardial infarction. The metaphor of the human heart as the home of emotions is so old we rarely question it. When you think about it, saying your heart has been broken is no less strange than the Japanese equivalent "to sever one's intestines."

Dead as a doornail.

Well and truly dead. Even Charles Dickens pondered why the language had seized upon that particular object. As he wrote in the opening to *A Christmas Carol*: "Old Marley was as dead as a door-nail. Mind! I don't mean to say that I know, of my own knowledge, what there is particularly dead about a door-nail. I might have been inclined, myself, to regard a coffin-nail as the deadest piece of ironmongery in the trade. But the wisdom of our ancestors is in the simile; and my unhallowed hands shall not disturb it, or the Country's done for. You will therefore permit me to repeat, emphatically, that Marley was as dead as a door-nail."

THIS IS AN EX-PARROT

English has many euphemisms for death. The British comedy team Monty Python rattled through many of them in a famous sketch in which John Cleese tries to return a dead parrot to a pet store run by Michael Palin who refuses the return insisting the bird is not dead, only sleeping. Here are the euphemisms: "deceased," "demised," "passed on," "ceased to be," "expired and gone to meet its maker," "late," "stiff," "bereft of life," "rests in peace," "pushing up the daisies," "run down the curtain," and "joined the choir invisible."

~ Around the World ~

For who's a prince or a beggar in the grave?
(Persian) You can't take it with you.

~ 79 ~
Regional Phrases

The English language is spread across the globe, and such a widespread tongue produces a multiplicity of wonderful varieties.

Another kick at the cat.

Canadian. Another attempt to get something done. It seems that this saying evolved in the Great White North when people misheard—or deliberately made a joke of—the phrase "another kick at the can," referring to the game kick the can. In its present version it calls to mind the expression "more than one way to skin a cat." (I would like to take this moment to ensure my international readers that English speakers are no more prone to animal abuse than anyone else. Really.)

Bless your heart.

This is an all-purpose phrase in the southern U.S. In its most basic form it is exactly what it seems to be, a blessing. A Southerner might utter it in response to good or bad news, if you got a promotion or were diagnosed with an illness. It can also be used in a patronizing manner, or to soften the blow when engaging in nasty gossip. "She's put on a few pounds, bless her heart."

Bob's your uncle.

British. Used to sum up something that is easy to do. (There is a joke about a Londoner giving directions to an American tourist, saying, "You just take the bus one stop and Bob's your uncle," to which the American replies, "Thank you, but how did you know my uncle was named Robert?") Before you ask, no one really knows who Bob is. Oh, there are stories. The *OxfordWords* blog of *Oxford Dictionaries* recounts one that it calls "beguiling" (i.e., "apocryphal," i.e., "probably totally made up"). But because there isn't a more documented origin, I will repeat the tale. Before he was prime minister of England, the young and inexperienced Arthur Balfour got himself appointed to a number of important posts because his uncle Robert Cecil (Lord Salisbury) was then himself prime minister. Everything is easy if Bob's your uncle. Of course, it's just as likely that the saying evolved out of an old slang expression "all is bob," which meant "everything is fine."

Inside baseball.

An American publisher recently rejected a proposal of mine by telling my agent it was "too much inside baseball." My agent, who is British, had no idea what they meant. "Inside baseball" is something that is highly detailed and specialist, like the conversation a coach would have in the locker room with the players, as opposed to the enjoyable experience of the spectators watching the game. It is conversation that is only understood by an in-group, much like this idiom.

Eye-power.
Singaporean. Said of someone who sits around watching other people do the work. "We've done all the heavy lifting. You have good eye-power, eh?"

Face like a dropped pie.
Australian. Ugly.

Fill your boots!
Canadian. Do it if it makes you happy. An American equivalent is "Whatever floats your boat."

Kangaroos loose in the top paddock.
Canadian. Just kidding. It's Australian. It refers to someone who is a bit crazy in an eccentric, harmless way.

Let me land.
Nigerian. Let me finish.

Living in high cotton.
U.S. South. From the cotton-growing land comes an expression that means you're doing very well, like a farmer when his crop is in full bloom.

FALSE FRIENDS

Our friends up north in Canada have a saying "bugger the dog," sometimes used with a more forceful verb. You might think this is a synonym for the expression "to screw the pooch," meaning to mess something up in a big way. In fact, it is not. "Buggering the dog" is to be slow or lazy.

Also beware of the expression "blow off." In American English this means to stand someone or something up. "Let's blow off that class and go shopping." In British English it is slang for passing gas. So when a Brit hears an American say, "He blew me off," that Monty Python catchphrase about "farting in your general direction" comes to mind.

Mad as a meat-ax.

Australian. Crazy.

Like a fart in a trance.

Scottish. A dreamy person. Someone who floats around ineffectively. In Iceland they might say, "You are completely out driving" (Þú ert alveg úti að aka) for a similar effect.

More grease to your elbow.

Nigerian. Bravo! Well done! A combination of the phrase "elbow grease" and the antiquated British expression "More power to your elbow." Applauding one's hard work.

Stone the crows!

Australian. An exclamation of surprise or amazement.

To suck out of one's thumb.

South African. It means to spout complete nonsense. Americans have a similar phrase, but we pull our nonsense out of another part of the anatomy. The phrase seems to have come to South African English via the Dutch, as they use almost the same expression. It also exists in Hebrew and Russian.

Too poor to paint and too proud to whitewash.

U.S. South. It describes someone down on his luck but not quite able to keep up appearances because of pride. Whitewash is cheaper than paint.

WHAT DID YOU JUST SAY?

Your Australian friend tells you he's "flat out like a lizard drinking." What do you respond?

A. "Call me back when you're sober."
B. "I can lend you a little until payday."
C. "I'll get back to you when you have more time."
D. "Huh?!"

ANSWER: D. Then after he explains himself, C. It means he's really busy. (If your non-Australian friend tells you this, the correct answer is A.)

~ 80 ~
The End

How the mighty have fallen.

Today this expression is usually used with irony or even undisguised glee after someone powerful and crooked has gotten his comeuppance. It comes from the Bible, and in its original context it is anything but celebratory. David, in spite of being persecuted by Saul, lamented the death of Israel's first king and his son Jonathan, saying, "How are the mighty fallen in the midst of battle! O Jonathan, thou wast slain in high places!" The Japanese have a colorful phrase for someone who has suffered this sort of fall from grace. "Once a sword," they say, "now a vegetable knife."

All over but the shouting.

The shouting is the applause. It means you are so certain of success that you're just waiting for the congratulations. The Welsh sportswriter Charles James Apperley used the line for the first time in print in 1905 in a description of a horse race. He was probably recording horse-racing slang as he heard it: "'It's all over but the shouting,' exclaims Lilly. 'Antonio's as dead as a hammer' . . . The trainer's figure of speech was not carried out to the letter. Antonio was not dead, but only dead beat."

That's all she wrote.

That's all there is. Discussion is closed. It evokes the image of woman writing a letter to her significant other to end the relationship. The phrase was popularized by its use in Texas Troubadour Ernest Tubb's 1942 song "That's All She Wrote." Etymologists have traced the origin of this phrase to the American South, but no one has any idea who "she" is.

Around the World

The Buddha's image is made, but the eyes have not been put in.

(Japanese) It lacks finishing touches.

Drawing the sword because this is the end.

(Japanese) As if there were no tomorrow.

Everything has an end, only the sausage has two.

(German: *Alles hat ein Ende, nur die Wurst hat zwei.*) All good things must come to an end.

DO YOU KNOW WHAT YOU'RE SAYING?

When phrases become fixed, people utter them without a lot of thought as to where they came from. Here are a few clichés to make you think twice.

COTTON-PICKIN'.

A mild epithet expressing annoyance. "Get that cotton-pickin' truck off my lawn!" Cotton-pickin' has some uncomfortable racial implications. Whether it is outright racist or not is a matter of semantic hairsplitting. Picking cotton is notoriously difficult, which is why that labor was, in the bad old days, assigned to slaves. To call someone a "cotton picker" was a racist insult. "Cotton-pickin'" is a little more complicated. Although it sounds older, it only appeared in a non-agricultural context for the first time in the 1940s. It was popularized by Bugs Bunny cartoons. Technically, in this version it is a reference to the difficulties of picking cotton itself, rather than a derogatory statement about the slaves who picked it. That's a distinction without a difference. It's best to avoid this one.

DRINKING THE KOOL-AID.

It means to accept an idea without question. Usually it is applied to someone fully adopting a company's culture. It is a reference to the 1978 mass murder/suicide of members of a religious cult called the Peoples Temple led by Jim Jones in which 918 people died.

INDIAN GIVER.

Someone who gives a gift only to take it back. This saying resulted from cultural misunderstanding between Native Americans and the European colonists. Rather than conducting trade with money, the Native Americans had a barter economy based on personal relationships. If I give you a gift, I assume you will repay me with a gift or a favor of similar value at some point. Expecting something in return for a gift went against European notions of fair play. It didn't occur to them that they might be just as guilty of breaking the locals' notions of fair play. As Lewis Hyde wrote in *The Gift*, "The opposite of 'Indian giver' would be something like 'white man keeper' . . . that is, a person whose instinct is to remove property from circulation."

SOLD DOWN THE RIVER.

This phrase, meaning to be cheated or betrayed, has its origins in the slave trade. It meant to buy a slave in an area with better working conditions, such as Virginia or northern Mississippi, and then to sell him down the river for the plantations in lower Mississippi, where conditions were much harsher. Maybe this is why this phrase is quickly being replaced by the cliché "To throw someone under the bus" (see p. 132).

TO GO POSTAL.

To go crazy, especially from overwork. This 1990s cliché is an allusion to a series of workplace shootings in the U.S. by postal workers (usually described as "disgruntled" in the media).

RESOURCES

WEBSITES

About World Languages: http://aboutworldlanguages.com

English Language and Usage: http://english.stackexchange.com

Language Log: http://languagelog.ldc.upenn.edu/nll/

New York Times "On Language": http://topics.nytimes.com/top/features/magazine/columns/on_language/index.html

Online Etymology Dictionary: http://www.etymonline.com/

Oxford Dictionaries: http://www.oxforddictionaries.com/us

Oxford English Dictionary: www.oed.com

The Phrase Finder: http://www.phrases.org.uk

Straight Dope: http://www.straightdope.com/

Word Detective: http://www.word-detective.com/

Word Origins: wordorigins.org

World Wide Words: www.worldwidewords.org

BOOKS

Akabio, Anietie. *The Sayings of the Wise: Ibibio Proverbs and Idioms*. Uyo: Marshall Press, 1900.

Arnanader, Primrose, and Ahkhain Skipwith. *The Son of a Duck Is a Floater*. London: Stacey International, 1993.

Barra, G. *1,000 Kikuyu Proverbs*. Nairobi: Kenya Literature Bureau, 2010.

Buchanan, Daniel Crump. *Japanese Proverbs and Sayings*. Norman: University of Oklahoma Press, 1965.

Burton, Richard. *Wit and Wisdom from West Africa*. London: Tinsley Brothers, 1865.

Calana, Zollie, and Patrick Holo. *Xhosa Proverbs and Metaphors*. Cape Town: Kwela Books, 2002.

Chang, Albert F. *Collection of Equivalent Proverbs in Five Languages*. Hamilton Books, 2012.

de Boinod, Adam Jacot. *Toujours Tingo*. New York; Penguin, 2010.

Dodson, Stephen, and Robert Vanderplank. *Uglier Than a Monkey's Armpit*. New York: Perigee Books, 2009.

Flonta, Teodor. *Dictionary of English and Romance Languages Equivalent Proverbs*. DeProverbia, 2011.

Funk, Charles Earle. *2107 Curious Word Origins, Sayings and Expressions*. New York: Galahad Books, 1993.

Habibian, Simin, K. *1001 Persian-English Proverbs*. Bethesda, MD: Ibex Publishers, 1995.

Hart, Henry. *100 Chinese Proverbs*. Stanford, CA: Stanford University Press, 1954.

Kizza, Immaculate N. *The Oral Tradition of the Baganda of Uganda*. Jefferson, NC: McFarland Publishers, 2010.

Kvetko, Pavol. *Slovak-English Dictionary of Idioms*. Iris, 1996.

Lipinski, Miroslaw. *Dictionary of 1000 Polish Proverbs*. New York: Hippocrene Books, 1997.

Owomoyela, Oyekan. *Yoruba Proverbs*. University of Nebraska Press, 2003.

Partridge, Eric. *Dictionary of Catchphrases*. London: Taylor & Francis, 2005.

Percival, P. *Tamil Proverbs*. New Delhi: Asian Educational Services, 1996.

Rees, Nigel. *The Cassell Dictionary of Word and Phrase Origins*. London: Cassell, 1999.

Rogers, James. *The Dictionary of Clichés*. New York: Wings Books, 1985.

Rohsenow, John. *ABC Dictionary of Chinese Proverbs*. Honolulu: University of Hawaii Press, 2002.

Safire, William. *William Safire's Political Dictionary*. New York: Oxford University Press, 2008.

Speake, Jennifer. *Oxford Dictionary of Proverbs*. London: Oxford University Press, 2008.

Wilson, Alan, et al. *They Have a Saying For It*. Gallup, NM: Hashke Publications, 2000.

INDEX

ABOUT THE AUTHOR

Laura Lee is the author of twenty books including the companion to *Around the World in 80 Clichés*, *Savior Faire*, a book of foreign phrases commonly used by English speakers. She is best known for her humorous reference books such as *The Pocket Encyclopedia of Aggravation*, *The Elvis Impersonation Kit*, *Blame it on the Rain*, and *Don't Screw It Up!* The *San Francisco Chronicle* has said of her work: "Lee's dry, humorous tone makes her a charming companion. . . . She has a penchant for wordplay that is irresistible."

In addition to humorous reference, she has written a children's book, *A Child's Introduction to Ballet*, two novels, *Angel* and *Identity Theft*, and the forthcoming biography *Oscar's Ghost*, which deals with conflicts between members of Oscar Wilde's circle over his legacy after the playwright's death.

Lee brings to her writing a unique background which includes work as a professional mime, improvisational comic, and radio announcer. After a three-year stint as a part-time touring public relations director for a Russian ballet company, Lee has returned to her native Michigan where she divides her time between writing and producing educational ballet tours with her partner, the Russian ballet dancer Valery Lantratov.